Hurry, Hurry, While Stocks Last

A sideways look at the economic, social
and shopping history of Cumbria
as seen through local advertisements
1850-1940

by

Hunter Davies

BOOKCASE

A BIT OF OLD KENDAL.—This is
ROBERT BLENKHORN'S SHOP, 7, & 9, Stramongate.

An Old Business Place full of New Goods.

DON'T FORGET THE ADDRESS:

ROBERT BLENKHORN,

IRONMONGER AND NAIL MANUFACTURER,

7, & 9, Stramongate, Kendal.

© Copyright Hunter Davies 2001
Published by Bookcase, 17 Castle Street, Carlisle CA3 8SY
Printed by Sadlers, Wigton, Cumbria CA7 9SJ
ISBN 1 904147 00 3

Contents

Biographical Note

Hunter Davies is the author of over 30 books, many of them with Cumbrian connections, such as *A Walk Around the Lakes* and biographies of Wordsworth, Wainwright, Beatrix Potter and, most recently, the one and only Eddie Stobart. He grew up and went to school in Carlisle and now divides half of each year between London and Loweswater. He is married to the Carlisle-born novelist and biographer, Margaret Forster.

APPOINTED PURVEYORS OF BISCUITS
TO H.M. KING EDWARD VII.

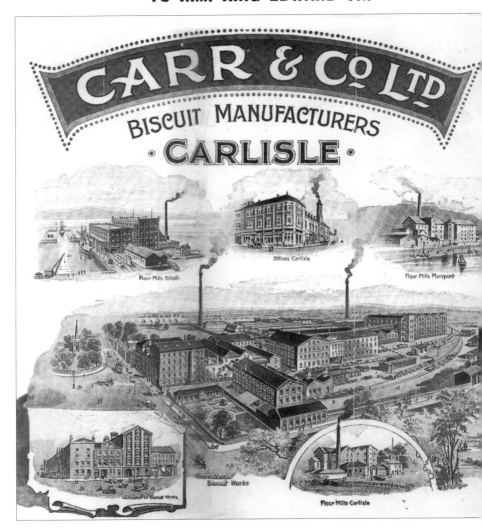

Appointed Biscuit Bakers to the late Queen Victoria
by Special Warrant 8ᵗʰ May 1841

By Way of Introduction

For over thirty years I've been collecting Cumbrian memorabilia and ephemera – books, newspapers, magazines, postcards, photographs, diaries, letters, leaflets, posters, letter-heads, cheques from dead Cumbrian banks, programmes from long-gone theatres, bills from forgotten businesses, tickets for events which will never happen again, any old paper rubbish really, as long as it is somehow connected with Cumbria and the Lake District.

As the years have gone by, flicking through my treasures, blowing off the dust to admire the detail, sometimes wondering why on earth I bought them, I've found myself more and more drawn to the advertisements rather than the contents. At the time, they were often the peripheral features, bottom of the page in the newspapers, stuck at the front or the back of old guidebooks or gazeteers, not meant or expected to be treasured for themselves. Yet I look at some of them for hours, pondering the prose, enjoying the typography, studying the art work, working out the unspoken signs and signals, watching the changes over the years.

With guide books we're buying information, with newspapers it's news and observation, both are attempting to reflect their times, telling us what is happening now, this moment. In the case of guide books, they also hope the contents will be so good that we'll keep them and use them for years. With advertisements, the object is much simpler. All they are saying is hurry, hurry, buy now, my pies are gorgeous, my hotel is excellent. They are not seeking to reflect what is happening in the wider world, in the next town, even the next street, only what they have stocked in their shop or on offer in their dining room. They expect you to read them once and then forget them.

Or, with advertising fliers, to bin them immediately.

But advertisements are also creatures of their age, of the language, attitudes, fashions and happenings which are currently around them. They record and provide information, often unwittingly, about a great deal of what was really going on in the lives of ordinary people.

Now why did I use the word 'gorgeous' back there? It just plopped out. 'Gorgeous' is an archaic adjective which is now back in common usage, quite smart, used recently in a popular song, but this time it has ironic undertones, half mocking what it describes. I smile when I hear it creeping out of my mouth. I mean it when I say 'It's gorgeous,' but I am also commenting on myself saying it. If someone were to think I'm being soppy and sentimental or overdoing it by saying 'gorgeous,' I can say, 'Heh, of course I am, I know I am.'

I have an advertisement in front of me from the 1880's in Penrith. It was in a give-away sheet called The Tradesmen's Local Advertiser which listed several local firms and their goods for sale. One of them is Herd Bros. They had a nursery in Penrith selling ornamental trees, trees, shrubs, roots, bulbs. At the end of the little advert it says, 'Catalogues and all information free by post. Get our lists and see our stuff if you can.'

FOREST TREES, Ornamental Trees and Shrubs, Hedge Plants, Fruit Trees
Carnations and Roses a speciality. The hardiest and best in cultivation.
WRITE FOR DESCRIPTIVE PRICE LIST
The " VILLA" collection of Bulbs (for indoor or outdoor) 21/- Half 10/6. Containing 850 grand Roots, delivered Carriage free. Catalogues and all information free by post.
Get our lists and see our stuff if you can.
HERD BROS., Victoria and Castle Nurseries, PENRITH.

The word 'stuff' jumped right out at me. It seems such modern slang, a word we all use and throw about today when we can't be bothered to list further items and ideas or anything really, we just use it, to save us thinking and all that stuff. In the 1880's I would have expected them to say 'Come and see our goods or items' not 'our Stuff'.

It's a minor example but typical of what makes me sit and ponder. Looking back we cannot always understand or translate the undertones and influences in words used in the past. Lines from songs, catchphrases in the air, often flourish and disappear without ever being properly pinned down. It's these changes in the use of words, and in style and presentation, which I find so fascinating.

From decade to decade, as life goes on, the products themselves, the goods and services which are on offer, all change, and so does the style of selling them to the public. This style, this mode of presentation, is equally part of the passing show.

They also reflect things peculiar to us here in Cumbria, reminding us of firms and shops and ways long gone, plus some still with us.

When I'm flicking through these advertisements, and time can hang heavy here in Loweswater when it's raining, I'm roughly looking out or being amazed by ten areas, ten elements in old Cumbria advertisements which catch my eye and which I consider to be jolly interesting. ('Jolly'- that's also ironic.)

VIGNETTES By vignettes I mean the illustrations in old ads, some photographic, some line drawings, often decorated with fancy scrolls and stuff. They can be so pretty and attractive, yet you never see such vignettes today. At one time, even the humblest butcher or manufacturer would have an elaborate illustration in his advertisement, on his bills and invoices and letter-heads, even on his cheques. Usually it showed a large photograph or drawing of his shop or premises, packed with his goods, his stuff proudly lined up. The bigger the firm the grander the display. When Carrs in Carlisle went national their advertisements were like the colour supplements, filled with buildings and factories, but even as a little bakery shop in Castle Street, they used little vignettes to advertise themselves.

I always buy old copies of The West Cumberland Times, now long gone, whenever I come across them, because their masthead illustration was so, well, gorgeous. It ran right across the top of the front page and showed a sailing ship, barrels, factories, chimneys, a large clock ticking away, sheep, cows, lakes. So much is crammed in, yet all is so artistic. Newspapers today, they slap their title at the top and that's it.

TYPOGRAPHY Along with the vignette this is what made old ads so attractive. Experts can date a typeface in an advert to within ten years. New typefaces were always coming in while old ones were discarded, considered out-of-date, giving the wrong image and impression.

The fashion in the mid-nineteenth century was to show off your typeface, display the whole range, let the world see how clever you were, or at least your compositor. You see it in old railway posters or theatre bills, when in the same advert they would have umpteen typefaces, going up and down in size and fanciness. It must have strained your eyes, made your head ache, trying to take it all in, the message being so massaged by the messenger.

Look over the page at that 1857 advert from a cement firm in Carlisle, one John Rushton. It runs to almost twenty lines, and in each line, the type is different in some way. It's more like a printer's brochure, to illustrate what he can do, rather than a list of the latest cements. (Portland Cement is still selling today,

WEST CUMBERLAND TIMES, NOVEMBER 20TH, 1927.

Wordsworth's Guide. 1851

but what happened to Florentine Cement and Roman Cement. Dead fashionable in Carlisle circa 1850's)

In the twentieth century advertisements went for cleaner, simpler, more modern type, using fewer varieties, but even so, the tendency was still there to add the fancy bit.

EXHORTATIONS Now we come to the language of advertisements. Firstly, let us consider their manners.

Back in the nineteenth century, they were ever so humble, so Uriah Heepish, falling over backwards to be polite. The vendor or shopkeeper was always begging leave to draw attention to his goods, humbly offering his services.

In !857, R.A.Holliday, a joiner of Scotch Street, Carlisle, announced that he was returning 'thanks to the public for the many favours conferred upon him since his commencement in

LIGHTING-UP TIME.
TO-DAY (Saturday), 4-38 p.m
Wednesday (Nov. 30th), 4-32 p.m

Wordsworth's Guide. 1851

business and begs leave to inform the Agriculturists and the Public generally that he still continues to supply Winnowing Machines.'

In 1880, James Lomas of Maryport, who had a boot, shoe and slipper establishment at Crosby Street, announced that 'he respectfully intimates to his numerous friends and customers that his Stock of Boots and Shoes is now complete and while heartily thanking them for past favours, he solicits a

continuance of that liberal support which they have always
afforded his stock . . .' Oh do get on with it, is how we'd react
to all that today.

Thomas Weeks, joiner and carpenter of Cross Hill, St. Bees,
intimated in 1891 that he has conducted business in the village
for some years and hopes for a continuance of first class
workmanship, punctuality and reasonable charges always to
merit support.'

By the twentieth century the dialogue between supplier
and customer had started to change. Self-effacement is out,
understatement and low-key whispering are no longer used.
Tradesmen have started to shout, judging by the arrival of so
many exclamation marks.

'YOUR PIANO REQUIRES TUNING!!!' shouted out loud a
large, underlined headline in 1900 from Henry Unsworth of 22,
Gillingate, Kendal. 'So it will interest you to know that if a
Piano is well tuned the consequent improvement adds 50% per
cent.' To the value of the piano or just its sound? I'm not clear
about that or the use of the three exclamation marks. Using a
question mark would seem a touch politer, as opposed to
accusing you of having a dodgy piano.

'LOOK HERE ! ! ' exclaimed the Kendal Window Cleaning

LOOK HERE ! !

 Don't you think it's time you had your Windows Cleaned ?

The Kendal Window Cleaning and Carpet Beating Company

Undertake this work at a very reasonable cost. Why risk your own, or your Servants Necks, especially during the perishing days of Winter, when, **by sending a Post Card** to the above Company, you can have the work done promptly and well.

When Spring Cleaning

don't forget to turn your Carpets out to the

Kendal Window Cleaning and Carpet Beating Co., 6, AYNAM PLACE, KENDAL.

and Carpet Beating Company. 'DON'T YOU THINK IT'S TIME YOU HAD YOUR WINDOWS CLEANED?' No nonsense there. Nor was the next line. 'Why risk your own or you Servants Necks especially during the perishing days of Winter.'

W, Oram, butchers, in Lowther Street, Carlisle, a firm I remember well, was, in 1911, proclaiming that they had enjoyed '50 years of supremacy in the worthy but difficult field of PURE FOOD PURVEYING. For 50 years, W. Oram and Sons have striven to so conduct their business so that no-one should even ask 'Is this good?' if he knew it came from Oram's.' What a boaster.

Henry McAleer, of Pow Street, Workington, who sold boots

and shoes, offered a £10 reward in 1900 to anyone who would wear out a pair of his porpoise skin boots in six months. Sounds more like a dare than a boast. His shop, so he went on, was 'the largest establishment in the North, the greatest choice, the smallest profit and the best value.' Covers everything, really.

One of his other slogans was a bit more complicated. 'Three pairs have been known to wear a middle-aged man the remainder of his life.' I think a bit of re-writing was needed there.

Porter's Postal Directory, 1882

15

In a Penrith directory for 1900 appeared an advert for a vaudeville show at the Hippodrome, Dalton Square, Lancaster. Their boasts were most re-assuring. 'Everything to please. Nothing to Offend. So bright, crisp, clean entertainment, entirely free from vulgarity,' which, of course, is what we all still want today.

ENDORSEMENTS are still with us. Only the personalities change. At one time, so they boasted, their celebrity customers included royalty and members of the aristocracy. Now it's footballers and T.V. stars who, I'm sure, are much more expensive.

Hotels loved to list the names of nobs in their advertisements, such as. The Royal Oak in Keswick. It was boasting in 1931 that 'this establishment has had the honour of receiving the patronage of the Late Queen Dowager, HRH the Prince of Wales, the King of Saxony, the Grand Duke Constantine of Russia, &c. &c.' I wonder if they all came at the same time? Must have been crowded. And did they pay for the testimonial or just let them off with the bill? Perhaps they waited till they were all late, dead and forgotten. Or they just made it all up.

Ordinary, local shops had to make do with anonymous quotes and references from letters sent to them, unsolicited, of course, by customers who had written in to rave, referred to only by their initials. Now and again they did manage endorsements from well known local personages, such as Harriet Martineau, the writer who lived in Ambleside. She seems to have been very free with her praises.

Cooper Brothers of Cockermouth, well known in their time for their lemonades, ginger beers and soda waters, clearly considered themselves very fortunate in securing the endorsement of Professor Wanklyn. 'Gentlemen, I have analysed the sample of Soda Water you sent me and also the Pump Water employed in making the Soda Water, and can report favourably on them. The water is organically clean and free from poisonous metals. It is well charged with Carbolic Acid and is Excellent Soda Water.' Professor Wanklyn? Oh, he was once very big in soda circles, allegedly.

POLITICS You wouldn't normally expect political references to infiltrate local adverts. No-one wants to upset customers, no matter what their political opinion, but they do occasionally creep in if they concern foreign politicians, who can be used or ridiculed from a safe distance.

In 1934, in the Wigton Advertiser, the County Laundry in Carlisle managed to drag into its advert one of the biggest political stories of the day – the rise of Fascism. But how, you may ask, did they manage to connect Fascism with cleaning clothes? No problem.

'Where Do the Black Shirts Go?' asks the headline. 'To the Laundry that knows how,' was the answer. Underneath the headline, just in case you didn't get the joke, there were mug shot drawings of Oswald Mosley, Mussolini and Hitler. Not very skillful drawings, but the political reference was smart.

SOCIAL CHANGES Advertisements, without meaning to, do give an insight into social conditions and attitudes of the day. References to servants were frequent right up to the last War, the implication being that most customers, of the sort most firms wanted, had at least one servant.

Throughout the nineteenth and the early twentieth centuries, it was common in West Cumbria to see references to emigrants and emigration. Not just the special offers for the steamships heading to America, one way only, but to items and products, trunks and clothes, which might be of use to those contemplating emigration. Which millions did of course, from West Cumbria, or passing through our West Coast ports on the way to a new life.

OLD THINGS NOW GONE You see things you never see any more, which are only remembered by older people. Very often, it's hard to work out precisely what they were, what they did.

Underhill, the butcher, in Highgate, Kendal, was in the 1930's selling ' brawns, polonies and home rendered lard.' I can work out what brawns were, and how lard was home rendered, but what were polonies? No, don't tell me. I'll just imagine it.

H. UNDERHILL,

Wholesale & Retail Pork Butcher,

187, HIGHGATE,

KENDAL.

MAKER OF HIGH-CLASS

BRAWNS, PIES, POLONIES, PUDDINGS, SAUSAGES, HOME-RENDERED LARD, &c.

NOTICE.—We Make all we Sell, and
- - Sell all we Make - -

Home-Cured Hams and Bacon from your own County Fed Pigs in Prime Condition. Ask our Prices.

Note Address—Near Abbot Hall.

History of Football in Kendal. 1908

Also in Kendal, Edward Hayton, spirit merchants, was acting as sole agent for 'Invalid Oatmeal Stout.' Never heard of that, but it sounds good, probably organic and dead healthy. I bet it would sell well today.

THE LATEST THINGS This is the life-blood of any shop, any merchant, being able to boast that he has the newest goods, the latest styles, the up-to-the-minute fashions.

Fashions matter most in women's clothes, from self-adjusting corsets to cycling frocks, yet it's surprising how rarely our Cumbrian shops boasted about having the latest 'London' fashions., though there used to be a Workington shop which boasted it had the equal of anything in Regent Street. Perhaps Cumberland and Westmorland was just too far away from London for most local traders to bother importing the latest from the West End, knowing it would hardly impress the good folks of Distington or Cleator Moor.

Hotels also felt they needed to be offering the latest services and amenities. You can trace the arrival of almost all modern innovations by a careful reading of hotel literature.

In 1897, the Red Lion Hotel in Carlisle made a point of its 'Good Stabling. Posting in All its Branches.' By posting, they meant stage-coach posting – but they were also good on mail posting and communication generally, pointing out they were near the Post Office and also had a phone, 'Telephone No.17' that was easy to remember, and a Telegraphic Address 'Red Lion Carlisle'.

When coaches and horses went out, in came garages, while inside, in the bedrooms and public rooms, came the wonders of electricity, modern heating and sanitation.

FUN AND HUMOUR The reference to Black Shirts was clearly a joke, but I can be equally amused by wild boasts or convoluted prose. I have a photograph over my desk in Loweswater of Walter Willson's grocery shop in Aspatria from the 1920's with some of the staff outside, standing in their

21

THE ABOVE IS A VIEW OF A PLACE WHERE
YOU GET
Anything Connected with Sport !

History of Football in Kendal. 1918

aprons. Above the front door it says 'SHOPS everywhere.'

It always makes me smile, if no-one else. The other day a neighbour was staring at it, unable to see why I'd given it such a prominent place. I pointed at 'SHOPS everywhere' and he said, so what? It was such a lie, I said. They had a branch in Cockermouth, as all locals well know, but did they have shops in Manchester, or London or Peking? Of course not. He still didn't think it was funny.

I also smile at a rather attractive advert from Atkinson and Griffin, the Westmorland Garage in Kendal, which shows a large photograph of its premises, all very busy and cluttered, with the caption, 'The above is a view of a place where you get ANYTHING CONNECTED WITH SPORT'. It's silly rather than funny. Must have taken the great brains of Atkinson and Griffin, clutching their pencils, furrowing their brows, some time before finally agreeing on the wording.

A lot of the fun to be had from old adverts is unintentional. My favourite is probably from Hudson, the Brewers in Kendal who were offering 'Farmers supplied in 18, 9 and 5 Gallon Casks.'

So those were the reasons behind my choice of advertisements. I haven't tried to find out who did them, as that is a study in itself, but I presume there must have been an early form of advertising agency, even in the 1850's judging by the repetition of certain phrases and lay-outs. In many cases printers would have helped to create the advertisement, suggest the typeface and the illustrations. There must also have been space-sellers, people who went round shops and hotels selling advertising space in guide books and newspapers. They probably suggested the form of words, based on what others were doing and claiming.

HUDSON & Co.,

BREWERS.

Farmers Supplied in 18, 9, and
. . 5-Gallon Casks. . .

History of Football in Kendal. 1908

I like to think the tradesmen had the final say. The list of goods and excitements were his or her own choice, arranged in a way they thought would best show off their own stock and their own taste, and appeal to their own customers.

I've arranged the advertisements in ten different sections, according broadly to the goods or services on offer.

They are all purely local, Cumbrian advertisements – from local tradespeople trying to sell themselves to the local populace. I have not included any national advertisements for nationally known products which, of course, were also appearing at the same time. The history of these is well known.

Our local offerings and creations have tended to be over-looked and un-regarded, yet they are part of our local social history. Time to give them an airing, once again.

If you come across any good ones yourself, send them to Steve Matthews of Bookcase in Carlisle, not to me. I've got loads.

Hunter Davies, Loweswater, August 2001.

Wordsworth's Guide. 1851

THE KESWICK HOTEL.

(LIGHTED BY ELECTRICITY.)   Most convenient for Tourists en route to or from Scotland.

This Hotel is pleasantly situated on an eminence overlooking the new Fitz Park, and commanding views
unsurpassed loveliness, including the principal Mountains of the District, and is within a few minutes' walk fro

Derwentwater. It is connected with the Railway Station by a covered way; porters attend all the Trains, and th
guests virtually alight at and depart from the Hotel. Spacious COFFEE and DRAWING ROOMS; also, late
added, a commodious and well-supplied READING-ROOM and a RECREATION-ROOM. The Kitchen
supervised by an experienced Chef. GOOD GOLF LINKS Free to Hotel Visitors. Passenger Elevator.

J. B. WIVELL, Lessee

ULLSWATER HOTEL, Patterdale, Penrith,

Is one of the largest and best situated first-class Hotels in the district for Families and Tourists, delightfully placed
the shores of Ullswater, within a few yards of the Steam Yacht Pier, and commands most charming and varied View

of the Lake and of the wild secluded glens and lofty rugged heights with which this picturesque and beautiful neighbou
hood is surrounded.   Helvellyn and Aira Force are in close proximity.
The Steam Yacht and Coaches start from the front of the Hotel several times a day.   Certified Sanitation.
Tel. Address: "Bownass, Glenridding."   **THOS. BOWNASS, Proprietor.**

Chapter One
Tourism and Hotels.

Lakeland tourism began around 1770, which coincidentally was the year of Wordworth's birth. He did so much to attract people to Lakeland by his lovely poetry and his excellent guide book, but he also moaned and groaned about the arrival of unwashed hordes from Lancashire whom he thought would not have the education and the cultivated tastes and sensitivity to appreciate his Lakeland. He also didn't care for the newly rich industrialists building holiday homes in Windermere and Grasmere, though he and his family eventually moved into one.

By the end of his life, Wordsworth was complaining that Lakeland had been ruined by tourism, that things were not as they were when he was a boy, two cries which have been heard constantly, almost on the hour, for the last two hundred years. Off-comers, especially, are very fond of saying it's all been ruined, hoping that barriers will be put up, toll gates imposed to keep out new people – new people very much like themselves.

I don't think tourism has ruined Lakeland, only changed things, around the edges. But Wordsworth was correct in saying that things were different when he was a lad. Until the middle of the eighteenth century outsiders never visited Lakeland. If they knew about it, which is unlikely, they imagined it as a land full of wild beasts, awesome crags and frightening legends. The first visitors looked on themselves as explorers feeling frightfully brave.

When the first guide books came to be written from the 1770's onwards, human guides were always recommended, so that you might avoid anything really horrid. Instructions were given as to what you should see. You were told which sites and situations were Picturesque – a favourite word in guide books and advertisements at the time. It was suggested that you should take a Claud glass with you, a special sort of mirror, in order to admire the landscape.

The early tourist hotels naturally made a big feature of their local Picturesque landscape which could be appreciated by discriminating guests. They made a feature of the ease of transport to and from their hotel and also the transport they could arrange for guests to visit the local beauty spots by carriages, gigs, phaetons, wagonettes and dog carts. By the 1850's, when our period begins, the railways have arrived but local transport was still pulled by horses.

The Keswick Hotel considered itself about the biggest and best in Lakeland, 'commanding views of unsurpassed loveliness' yet connected directly with the railway station where porters would be on hand 'attending all trains.'

In Keswick itself, the Queen of the Lakes Pavilion and Refreshment Rooms claimed to be able to seat '500 at once for breakfast' while ' Fish, Ham, Eggs, Chops or Steak was available at the shortest notice. 'Imagine arriving out of the blue with a party of 500 and demanding a full English breakfast, at once. I can't think of anywhere in Lakeland where you could do that today.

As the century progressed hotels acquired telegraph communication and then telephones, but the biggest modern amenity was electricity. It transformed hotels in every sense. In 1931 the Victoria Hotel in Buttermere (now the Bridge Inn) was boasting about its Electric Light, hot and cold running water, free baths including a warm douche.'

FREDERICK RAPLEY,

Globe Family and Commercial Hotel and Posting House,

MAIN STREET, COCKERMOUTH.

This old-established and comfortable Hotel is replete with every comfort for the convenience Commercial Men and Families. Visitors to Cockermouth will find every comfort combined h moderate charges. Dog Carts, Brakes, and Carriages of every description, on the shortest ice, on Hire.

Porter's Postal Directory. 1882

"PRINCE CHARLIE'S" RESTAURANT AND TEMPERANCE HOTEL.

Mrs. E. Thompson, Proprietress,
Baker and Confectioner,
Devonshire Street, Penrith.

CYCLE TOURING CLUB QUARTERS.

THE increased popularity of temperance hotels throughout the country may be accounted for by the preference which many persons have for the cleanliness and quietude usually found in such establishments. The above well-known house, which "Prince Charlie" made his headquarters in 1745, was taken over about fifteen years ago by the present proprietress, and has amply demonstrated the need which existed for such an establishment in the town. The situation is central, and within ten minutes' walk from the railway station. The accommodation includes a comfortable and well-furnished sitting-room, dining-room, and well-aired bedrooms, bath-room, and lavatories, the sanitary arrangements being excellent. There is also special accommodation for cyclists. The food and cooking leave nothing to be desired, and the service is of the best. Tea and refreshments are provided on the shortest notice, the proprietress, who is ably supported by her two daughters, specially studying the comfort of her guests and patrons. The confectionery department displays a tempting assortment of most appetising quality of cakes, etc. All the leading confectionery and chocolate manufactures are represented in the stock, and

Mrs. Thompson is noted for her "own make" of brown bread. Cyclists and tourists may with confidence be commended to bestow their support upon this well-kept and neatly-ordered establishment.

YOUNGHUSBAND'S TEMPERANCE HOTEL,
Station Street, Keswick.

ESTABLISHED over twenty-nine years ago, and now carried on by the Misses S. and A. J. Younghusband, the above institution is one of the best-known of its kind in the Lake District. The house occupies a central and agreeable position and is replete with every modern convenience for commercial gentlemen and visitors. Its convenience as regards situation can be seen when it is said that the distance from the Station is only three minutes, and from the Lake (Derwentwater) only five. There are fifteen pleasant bedrooms, a commodious dining-room, a particularly agreeable sitting-room, with excellent bath rooms, and perfect sanitary arrangements. The cooking, service, etc., are of the best, and the comfort of the guests is strictly attended to. Cyclists and tourists generally are specially catered for. The terms are exceedingly reasonable when the excellence of the accommodation is considered. A shop for the supply of general groceries and confectionery is also carried on by the management. The connection is well-established, guests coming from all parts of the country and not infrequently making the house their headquarters for many years in succession.

During the Victorian era there was a growth in Temperance hotels which sprang up all over Lakeland. They tended to be relatively small and modest, aimed at hearty folks like cyclists and real walkers. By the look of their advertisements, some of them were rather austere and forbidding, not to say grim, such as Younghusband's Temperance Hotel in Keswick and Prince Charles Restaurant and Temperance Hotel in Devonshire Street, Penrith. The bigger ones did at least have some mod. cons. The Viaduct Temperance Hotel in Carlisle had 60 bedrooms, a billiards room and provided 'Boots meets Trains.' They also had a separate room for ladies. I'm surprised that non-drinking ladies felt the need to be kept apart from non-drinking men.

You hardly come across Temperance hotels today, anywhere. I supposes a modern equivalent would be our vegetarian hotels, mostly rather small, which are increasingly popular in Lakeland today, catering for much the same sort of healthy, good-living folk.

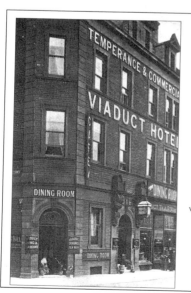

Carlisle Directory, Beaty 1924

There were not so many advertisements for specific tourist attractions in the nineteenth century, apart from the hotels and their associated amenities. You didn't have the tourist traps of today like animal parks, aquariums, the World of Beatrix Potters. But there was the celebrated Joseph Flintoff. Mr Flintoff arrrived in Keswick in 1823 and spent the next six years building a three-dimensional relief model of the whole of Lakeland complete with all the mountains and lakes. In most local guide books from the 1850's to the 1870's you'll see his full page advertisement, with quotes from famous people who had been impressed by his model. It was definitely a novelty, to be able to view the whole of Lakeland, and proved as popular, and no dafter, than paying to look at mock-ups of Beatrix Potter's lovely animals.

It wasn't cheap. In 1850, he was charging one shilling a visit. By 1860, he had changed it to 'one shilling each for each

WHEN IN CARLISLE CALL AT

BEATY'S, 98 English Street,

TWO MINUTES FROM STATION.

. . FOR . .

Luncheons, Teas, Etc.

Everything Best Quality.

Prices Moderate.

season'. Which meant, presumably, you could come back every day while you were on holiday. Somewhere to go, out of the rain. Not of course that it rained in the olden days. Oh no. It was always sunny then.

Flintoff's model was bought by the Keswick Lecture Society in 1878 for £160. You can still see it today, on show in the Keswick Museum. Hurry.

ANGLERS' INN,

ENNERDALE LAKE.

MR. FRANCIS NEWELL

Begs to inform the Gentry, Tourists, Anglers, and the Public generally, that he has recently obtained a Lease of the above-mentioned Premises, with the Lakes and Fell Becks belonging thereto; and having extended the accommodation, and re-furnished the Hotel, at considerable expense, F. N. trusts, by strict attention to the wants of his customers, and moderation in his charges, to command a share of their patronage.

WELL-AIRED BEDS.

Carriages, Post Horses, Boats (New), &c.,

ALWAYS IN READINESS.

WINES, SPIRITS, &c., OF THE BEST QUALITY.

ST. BEES, CUMBERLAND,
AS A HOLIDAY RESORT.

The "Manchester City News," of Aug. 12th, contained a contribution under this ad, signed W.J.P., from which the following extracts are taken :—

'A few weeks ago I set off to reconnoitre the West Coast of Cumberland as a holiday resort. The casual inspection of the coast led me to stay a couple of days at St. Bees, and the little place impressed me so favourably that I have just completed there one of the pleasantest, most restful, and beneficial holiday I have ever spent. One hardly obtains sufficient knowledge of a place in three weeks to become an authority on it, but it takes less time than to be quite sure that St. Bees is one of the most perfect little natural health resorts that lies within reach of Manchester. There is a capital bay ; the sands in this bay are clean, firm, and level, affording as safe a bathing place as I have ever seen. The sea is the principal attraction, as it rolls in from the Atlantic, but it is by no means the only one. The walks inland are in most directions very beautiful. The villages of Rottington, Coulderton, Beckermont, and the hill walks are intensely beautiful. The flora of the district is particularly varied. It may be thought that these natural advantages may be counter-balanced by disadvantages. I did not find it so. The water is exceptionally good ; practically absolute pure distilled water."

CIRCULAR TOURS BY RAIL AND WAGGONETTE TO THE LAKES.
TOURIST TICKETS FROM ALL PARTS.
TWO POSTAL DELIVERIES AND DESPATCHES, TELEGRAPH AND TELEPHONE OFFICES.

THE VISITORS' COMMITTEE WILL BE PLEASED TO GIVE ANY INFORMATION ON APPLICATION TO

THE SECRETARY, VISITORS' COMMITTEE, ST. BEES.

Whitehaven News County Annual 1900

Jenkinson's Guide 1872

CLOUDSDALE'S

CROWN HOTEL,

BOWNESS, WINDERMERE.

PATRONISED BY THE ROTHSCHILDS.

Parties visiting Windermere will find THE CROWN a First-class Hotel, conducted on modern principles, commanding uninterrupted Views of Windermere and the Mountains, and offering to Home and Foreign Tourists advantage of situation seldom possessed by any similar Establishment.

Families Boarded for Periods of not Less than a Week.

"I am quite satisfied at the moderation of your charges, as I was before of the comfort of your house."—*Harriet Martineau.*

"The Crown has Ten Private Sitting Rooms, and makes up Ninety Beds. Nothing can well excel the beauty of the view from its garden seat."—*Harriet Martineau.*

POSTAL TELEGRAPH.

We understand that the postal telegraph has been placed in CLOUDSDALE'S CROWN HOTEL, WINDERMERE. It will doubtless prove a great boon to merchants and others, as this is an exceptional instance of telegraph wires being affixed to private property for the public convenience.—*Westmoreland Gazette.*

THE CROWN HOTEL INFORMATION GUIDE, containing Map of the Lakes, Hotel, Hotel Tariff, Excursion Routes, Railway, Coach, and Steamboats Time Tables, &c., sent post free on application.

GRAND HOTEL, WHITEHAVEN.

MANAGERESS-MRS. HECKLE.

THREE FIRST-CLASS HOTELS.

THE GRAND HOTEL,	THE IMPERIAL HOTEL,	GREAT CENTRAL HOTEL,
WHITEHAVEN.	LIVERPOOL.	CARLISLE.

THESE three Hotels are worked in connection with each other, and rooms may be secured and arrangements made for visiting any of them on application to the respective managers.

Each Hotel is newly and handsomely furnished, and replete with every modern appliance. The comfort and convenience of visitors is made a matter of most careful study and attention, so that they may feel "At Home from Home."

BROOK HOUSE,

BOOT S.O.,

✶➤⚓ CUMB.

APARTMENTS.

EXCELLENT ACCOMMODATION FOR

TOURISTS AND VISITORS.

BROOK HOUSE is Large and Commodious, and Delightfully Situated near the Head of the Vale, among the Finest Mountain Scenery, a short distance from Stanley Ghyll Waterfall, and the Foot of Scawfell.

REFRESHMENTS PROVIDED.

PIC-NIC AND PLEASURE PARTIES CATERED FOR.

CYCLISTS WILL FIND THIS AN EXCELLENT RESORT.

HARRISON GAINFORD, Proprietor.

Whitehaven News County Annual 1900

WHITE HORSE INN,

PENRITH.

Wines and Spirits of the Choicest Brands

ALWAYS ON HAND.

Every accommodation for Commercial Travellers and others.

LICENSED TO LET

Carriages, Dog Carts, Gigs, Phaetons, Wagonettes

And all kinds of Conveyances.

N.B. W. T. begs to inform the Public that he has a First-class New HEARSE added to his Stock of Conveyances, and can furnish Funerals with Mourning Coaches and Attendants.

Directory 1899

FURNESS RAILWAY.

Twenty Coach and Steam Yacht Tours

THROUGH ENGLISH LAKELAND

DAILY during JUNE, JULY, AUGUST and SEPTEMBER.

No. 1.—**Outer Circular Tour,** embracing Windermere Lake, Furness Abbey, and Coniston.—Fare from 5/3.

No. 2.—**Inner Circular Tour,** embracing Furness Abbey, Coniston Lake (Gondola), and Crake Valley.—Fare from 3/3.

No. 3.—**Grange and Windermere Circular Tour,** embracing Grange, Arnside, Kendal, and Windermere Lake.—Fare from 2/9.

No. 4.—**Middle Circular Tour,** embracing Windermere Lake, the Crake Valley, and Coniston Lake. —Fare from 5/9.

No. 5.—**Red Bank and Grasmere Tour,** *via* Ambleside and Skelwith Force, returning *via* Rydal Water.— Fare from 2/9.

No. 6.—**Thirlmere, Grasmere, and Windermere Tour,** *via* Ambleside, Clappersgate, and Red Bank, and round Thirlmere Lake. — Fare from 5/-.

No. 7.—**The Four Lakes Circular Tour,** viz., Coniston, Grasmere, Rydal, and Windermere.—Fare from 5/9.

No. 8.—**Coniston to Coniston Tour,** *via* Red Bank, Grasmere, and Ambleside, returning by Coach to Coniston.—Fare from 4/6.

No. 9.—**Tarn Hows Tour,** *via* Ambleside and Coniston, returning by Tilberthwaite and Elterwater.—Fare from 4/6.

No. 10.—**Round the Langdales and Dungeon Ghyll Tour,** *via* Ambleside, Colwith Force, Grasmere, and Rydal.—Fare from 5/-.

No. 11.— **Ullswater Tour,** *via* Ambleside, Kirkstone Pass, and Brothers Water, returning *via* the Vale of Troutbeck and Lowwood. —Fare from 5/6.

No. 12.— **Derwentwater (Keswick) Tour,** *via* Ambleside, Grasmere, and Thirlmere.—Fare from 6/-.

No. 13.—**The Five Lakes Circular Tour,** viz., Windermere, Rydal, Grasmere, Thirlmere, and Derwentwater.—Fare from 11/6.

No. 14.—**Wastwater Tour,** *via* Seascale and Gosforth.—Fare from 4/6.

No. 15.—**The Six Lakes Circular Tour,** viz., Windermere, Rydal, Grasmere, Thirlmere, Derwentwater, and Ullswater. — Fare from 12/-.

No. 16.—**Duddon Valley Tour,** *via* Broughton-in-Furness, Ulpha, and Seathwaite.—Fare from 3/9.

No. 17.—**The Round of Coniston Lake (New Tour).**— Fare from 3/9.

No. 18.—**Ennerdale Lake and Calder Abbey** *via* Seascale, Gosforth, and Cold Fell.—Fare from 4/6.

No. 19.—**Across the Ferry Tour,** *via* Lake Side, Esthwaite Water, Hawkshead, and Storrs Hall.— Fare from 3/6.

No. 20.—**Cartmel Priory and Newby Bridge Tour,** *via* Windermere (Lake Side), Backbarrow Falls, Holker Park, and Grange.—Fare from 3/-.

For further particulars see "**Tours through Lakeland**" Pamphlets, to be had gratis at all Furness Railway Stations ; of Mr. F. J. RAMSDEN, Superintendent of the Line, Barrow-in-Furness ; at Messrs. THOS. COOK & SONS ; and the Polytechnic Institute, Regent Street, W. ; or Messrs. W. H. SMITH & SONS' principal Bookstalls. Price ½d.

Barrow with Fleetwood for Blackpool.—During the Summer months the Furness Railway Company's Paddle Steamers "Lady Margaret" or "Lady Evelyn" will run daily between Barrow and Fleetwood for Blackpool. Full particulars as to Sailings, Fares, &c., may be obtained on application to the Superintendent of the Line, Barrow-in-Furness ; or from Messrs THOS. COOK & SONS' Manchester, Blackpool, and other Agencies.

The Palette Album, illustrating the above Tours, in colours, can be obtained at the principal Railway Bookstalls, price 6d.

Picture Postcards of the Lake District may be obtained at any station on the Furness Railway, and on the Company's Steamers ; also at Furness Abbey Hotel and the principal Bookstalls. Reduced price, 12 cards for 6d.

ALFRED ASLETT,

Barrow-in-Furness, April, 1904.   Secretary and General Manager.

Chapter Two

Transport

Lakeland's first railway arrived in Windermere in 1848. It hadn't come far, only from Oxenholme and Kendal, but it had been hoped it would go much further, up and over Dunmail Raise and into Keswick. That was the original plan of the promoters. Wordsworth had soon put a stop to that writing letters of complaint and poems of protest. He didn't want this horrible thing going past his front gate at Rydal, spoiling his view, his peace and his quiet. 'Is there no nook of English ground secure from rash assault.' So he wrote. Could Wordsworth have been the first NIMBY?

But it did arrive on the shores of Lake Windermere and had an immediate effect. Its terminus was the lakeside hamlet of Birthwaite – which soon turned itself into a brand new town, calling itself Bowness. Combined with neighbouring Windermere, which was always there, slightly inland. Windermere is still Lakeland's biggest settlement.

There were soon railways all over Cumbria. At one time Carlisle had seven different railway companies running into the city. Only London had more. The Maryport and Carlisle went down the West Coast. The Lancaster and Carlisle went down the middle. The Midland Railway went on that remarkable route over to Settle. The Furness Railway, which opened in Barrow in 1846, dominated the south of Lakeland, but it never got past Coniston.

The only railway which eventually went through the heart of Lakeland was the Cockermouth, Keswick and Penrith Railway. It opened in 1865 and managed to bisect the Lakes, from West to East. This was the railway on the doorstep of the Keswick Hotel, very handy for its boots and porters, with its own private access. The line closed, alas, in 1972, though there are rumours about it being opened again, one day, soon.

Before the railways, it was possible to travel in and around Cumbria by water – not just on the open sea, but by canal. The Carlisle Navigation Canal opened with huge excitement and expectations in 1823. Along this canal travelled George Stephenson's Rocket in 1829, bound for Liverpool and for history.

Port Carlisle, at the entrance to the canal on the Solway, was a brand new creation, expected to be a major port and tourist attraction. In an advert in 1851, the Navigation Canal, offering Steam Packets to Liverpool described 'Port Carlisle being a place of great resort, good baths being established there.'

When the railways arrived they made a brave attempt to link in with railway timetables, but it didn't work. The railway killed off the Carlisle Navigation Canal, as it did canals elsewhere. It was abandoned in 1853. This advert, dated 1851, was about their last valiant attempt to drum up business.

But steam ships, sailing from Barrow, Whitehaven and

CARLISLE
CANAL NAVIGATION.

The Directors of the Carlisle Canal Company solicit the attention of the public to their Canal as a THROUGH MODE OF CONVEYANCE FOR GOODS AND PASSENGERS in connection with the Newcastle and Carlisle Railway, and Carlisle and Liverpool Steam Navigation Company.

For the Convenience of Shipping, the Channel of the Solway Frith is efficiently Lighted and Buoyed as recommended by Captain C. G. Robinson, R.N.

The Canal is 8 feet 6 inches deep; the Locks 72 feet 6 inches long, and 18 feet 4 inches wide.

Passage Boats Ply upon the Canal

To suit the Arrivals and Departures of the Steam Packets to and from Liverpool.

Port Carlisle being a place of great resort, (good Baths being established there), the Company Ply their Passage Boats during the Summer Months at Reduced Fares.

For further Information, as to Dues, &c., apply to

Mr. WILLIAM WARD,
CANAL OFFICE, CARLISLE,

ULLSWATER.

✦ "The English Lucerne." ✦

THE ROYAL MAIL STEAM YACHTS

Of the Ullswater Steam Navigation Co., Limited, will ply on Lake Ullswater (weather permitting and Sundays excepted), from Easter to end of September.

STEAMBOAT FARES.

Between			Single Fare. 1st Cl.	2nd Cl.	Return Fare. 1st Cl.	2nd Cl.
Pooley Bridge and Howtown	...		1 0	0 9	1 6	1 3
Howtown and Patterdale	...	...	1 6	1 0	2 0	1 6
Pooley Bridge and Patterdale		...	2 0	1 6	3 0	2 0

Children under 12, half price.

Pleasure Parties of not less than **Ten** will be taken at **Half Return Fare** for the double journey, on **one day's notice** being given to the Secretary or Captain, except by the boats leaving Patterdale at 1.40 p.m., and Pooley Bridge at 3.0 p.m. Season Tickets, £1. Weekly Tickets, first class, 6s. 6d. ; second class, 4s. 6d. Not transferable.

COACH FARES.

Between Penrith and Pooley Bridge : Single Tickets, 2s. ; Return Tickets, 2s. 6d. (Coachman's Fee included.)

Coaches for Ullswater leave Ambleside, Bowness, and Windermere, daily during the season. Fares from Ambleside : Single, 3s. 6d. and 4s. ; Return, 5s.

From Bowness and Windermere : Single, 6s. ; Return, 8s. 6d.

Fares from Ullswater (Patterdale) to Ambleside : Single, 5s. ; Return, 6s. 6d.

The following railways afford communication with Ullswater by Express Train Service to Penrith (the station for Ullswater), viz. :—London & Nor. West. Ry. ; Caledonian Ry. ; Nor. East. Ry. ; Midland Ry. (*via* Appleby) ; Gt. North. & Gt. East. (*via* York and Darlington) ; and the Gt. West. Ry., Lanc. & York Ry., Gt. Cent. Ry., Nor. Brit. Ry., Glas. & S. West. Ry., in conjunction with the L. & N. W. Ry.

TOURIST AND WEEK-END TICKETS TO PENRITH are issued at the principal stations of the above lines. The holders of Tourist Tickets to Scotland on the L. & N. W. System are allowed to break their journey (either way) at Penrith, in order to visit Ullswater.

CIRCULAR TOUR TICKETS, embracing Ullswater, are issued on C. K. & P. (from Keswick and Cockermouth), and L. & N. W. and Furness Railways. For particulars of which see the Railway Company's Tourist Programme.

GUIDE TO ULLSWATER. Maps and numerous Illustrations.
Post free, 7½d.

HOTEL AND LODGINGS GUIDE. Illustrated. 1½d.

For further information see the Company's Time Tables and Sailings Bill, or apply to

WILLIAM SCOTT, SECRETARY, Public Offices, Penrith.

Baddeley's Thorough Guide 1909

Maryport, out on the open seas, continued to do great business throughout the nineteenth century and the early twentieth century - taking coal and iron, finished goods as well as passengers, over to the Isle of Man and Ireland, down to London or across the Atlantic.

The emigration packages were aimed at those going off for good, to Australia, Canada and South Africa. Lots of inducements were thrown in. J.J.Wilson, licensed passenger broker of Egremont, headlined his advert in the 1890's with the words 'GOLD FOR ALL'. Thos. Meageen, authorised passenger broker of Whitehaven, was offering 'Free Homesteads and farms of 160

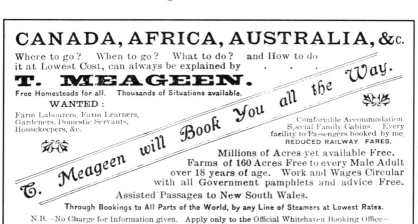
Whitehaven News County Annual 1900

acres free.' They were targeting 'farm labourers, farm learners, gardeners, domestic servants'. How could they resist when there were few opportunities at home.

Advertisements aimed at emigrants continued right up to the Second World War, but by then the word emigrant seemed to have fallen out of favour. In 1930, Pearson and Vipond, shipping and travel agents of Carlisle, were aiming their adverts at settlers, not emigrants.

46

Around the turn of the century, motoring arrived in its various forms - motor buses, motor bikes, motor cars. Garages opened in most towns and villages.

Some of these garages are still going to this day, such as County Garage in Carlisle, and so are some of the models. But most have long gone from the forecourts. Humber and Austin which were on sale from Dias and Co. in Carlisle in 1914, I can remember them well. But what was a Belsize car? Never heard of that one.

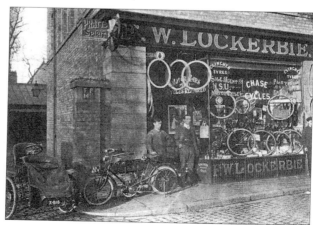

PURE HOME-MADE CONFECTIONERY.

DANIEL QUIGGIN,
WHOLESALE CONFECTIONER & SUGAR BOILER,
86, STRICKLANDGATE,
AND
25, ALLHALLOWS LANE,
KENDAL.

- All Sweets are Guaranteed Pure and are Sold -
- - - at the Lowest Prices. - - -

Mint Rock, Butter Drops, and Butter Toffee a Speciality.
Our Cream and Treacle Toffee is Delicious.

Try QUIGGIN'S "MONA" DROPS for Winter Use.

SHOPS SUPPLIED ON THE BEST TERMS.

Chapter Three
Food and Drink

We all need food and drink, always have done, so shops supplying us with such delights have been with us for centuries, most of them small scale and individual, with stuff cooked and baked, rendered and even killed on the premises. They often offered local delicacies, long forgotten or whose names have changed.

What were standing pies? That was what was on sale at John Ritson's confectionery establishment in Fisher Street, Carlisle in 1851. Mr. Ritson's foodshop was also the General Register Office for Respectable Servants. A strange combination, but apparently common at the time. Anthony Shaw, in the same street, also offered groceries and servants, as did John Little around the corner in Castle Street. You'd go into these establishments, ask for a standing pie, some sausages, some brides' cake, then say,'Oh, while I'm at it, I'll take a couple of your respectable servants.' I presume the connection was because cooks and kitchen staff made up a high proportion of the servant classes, so a bakers or grocers was a good place where they could be contacted.

Brides' Cake and Confectionery Establishment, No. 27, FISHER STREET, CARLISLE,
(LATE MRS. HORNSBY.)

JOHN RITSON

Begs leave very respectfully to return his most grateful Acknowledgments to the Nobility, Gentry, and the Public in general, for the patronage he has been favoured with during the Three Years he has been in the above Establishment; and further begs to state that he continues to make, on the shortest notice, Bride's Cake and Confectionery of every description.

Mrs. R. having had the Management of her Aunt's (Mrs. HORNSBY) Business for upwards of Fifteen Years, he (Mr. R.) can confidently recommend all he deals in to be of the same sterling quality that gave to Mrs. HORNSBY's Establishment so much celebrity.

STANDING PIES MADE TO ORDER.

☞ *General Register Office for Respectable Servants.*

Wordsworth's Guide. 1851

Brides' Cakes, with an apostrophe at the end, were, I assume, wedding cakes, but in another advert, wedding cakes as well as brides' cakes were listed - so were they the same or different? Questions, questions.

'DO WE ASK TOO MUCH?' was the question being asked

by Joseph Isaac Fisher of Duke Street, Whitehaven, in the1890's. He was a specialist, so he said, in high class provisions and was asking the world to compare his prices on butter, bacon and cheese. 'A fair trial is all we need.'

I was surprised to see margarine on sale in 1914. The Carlisle Bread Company was reporting 'an enormous demand for Daystar Margarine' which has 'the smallest proportion of

Carlisle Directory, 1914

moisture' It was made 'automatically in Silver Lined Vessels wrapped in Parchment by Electric Machines.'

Grocers and butchers were very fond of boasting that they had electricity. John Bell, in Botchergate, in Carlisle, in 1914, clearly felt he was bang up-to-date with his 'Minced Beef by Electric Motor.'

All sorts of exotic coffees and China Teas were available. Even in fairly out of the way places such as Brampton, you could find West Indian rums and French wines.

Carlisle Directory, 1914

But judging by the adverts, the most popular drink in Cumbria was aerated water. It came in various forms from ginger beer to sodas. Its popularity was partly connected with the Temperance Movement. All their members knew that strong drink was raging, wine a mockery.

All over Cumberland and Westmorland, little local companies were manufacturing and selling their own non-intoxicating aerated drinks, competing to be the purest, the fizziest. Almost all of them are gone today, just like the hundreds of small breweries who produced the harder stuff.

All shops tried to make their offerings look as attractive as possible. In real life and in their photographs, arranging their products to the best advantage, posing their staff in their best pinnies and aprons. One of the advantages in being in the confectionery and grocery line is that your shop always looked and smelled so good.

Daniel Quiggin in Kendal, still going strong today, showed his delivery horse and waggon in front of his shop, carrying another load of Pure Home-Made Confectionery. In that 1900 advert, they don't even mention Kendal Mint Cake.

According to Kendal Mint Cake history, Kendal Mint Cake

was first created in 1869 by one of Quiggin's Kendal rivals, Joseph Wiper. Quiggin didn't apparently add mint cake to their delights till 1920, but in 1900 they did have something called Quiggin's 'Mona Drops - for Winter Use'. I quite fancy some of them. But too late now.

JOHN SEVERS

FISH MERCHANT

AND

RABBIT SALESMAN.

47, HIGHGATE,

KENDAL.

**PRIMEST QUALITY OF FISH
A SPECIALITY.**

History of Football in Kendal 1900

57

RDEN SEEDS, BIRD SEEDS, POULTRY FOODS, DOG BISCUITS, MAPLE PEAS, TICK BEANS, MIXED CORN, BUCKWHEAT, TARES, &C.

SPECIAL MIXED SEED FOR CANARIES, LINNETS, &c.

👉 STEELE'S PARROT FOOD

In 2d., 4d., and 6d. sizes, is the Best Food in the World for this tribe of Birds.

ONIC SALINE SHELL GRIT, for Cage-Birds, Parrots, Pigeons, and Poultry.

EEP SALVE, DIP, GREASE, BUTTER, TAR, SULPHUR.

FT SOAP in 14lb Zinc Pails, 3s ; 28lb, 5s 6d ; Firkins, 9s 6d each.

ELE's Improved *LIQUID DIP* is the Best and Cheapest Summer Dip. 3s 9d per gallon, for 100 small sheep.

ELE's *PASTE DIP* for Wintering ; gives splendid results. 4s 6d per gallon, for 50 sheep ; 10s 6d per 2½ gallon bucket for 125 sheep.

ENT FOR M'DOUGALL'S, M'LEOD'S, JEYES', BANKHALL, AND ROBERTSON'S DIPS :—VENETIAN RED ON HAND.

ILET and *WASHING SOAPS* of all kinds. *SODA, DRY SOAPS,* &c.

mporter of Ceylon Teas

A Specialty, in which I offer packed in 20lb Boxes at 1s 7d per lb. Less Quantities, 1s 8d.

Y NOTED BLEND NO. 5, at *2s* (in 7lb and 20lb Tins at 1s 10d) Makes most delicious Cup, and is the Best Family Tea in the Kingdom. Try a 7lb Tin, it will speak for itself.

inest Pure Lard

In 28lb Buckets at Market Prices.

GROCERIES of all Kinds, Wholesale and Retail.

J. G. STEELE,

40, Market Place, Whitehaven.

Whitehaven News County Annual 1896

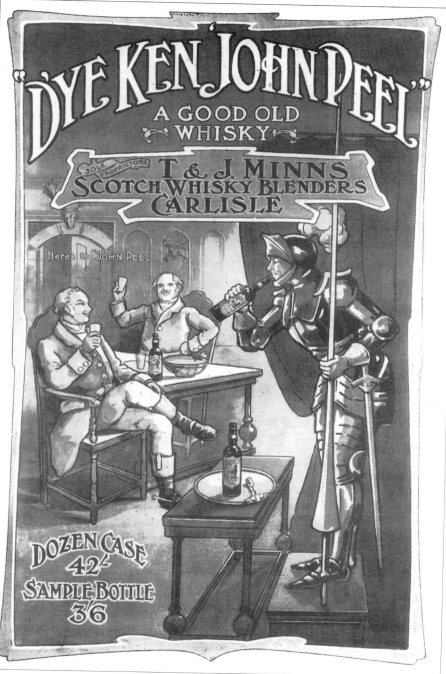

George Tweddle, Jun.

New Address: 26 Devonshire St.,

Ḣatter, Furrier, Glover.

Christy's and Lincoln Bennett's Hats, Dent's Gloves, Umbrellas,
Travelling Rugs, Shirts, &c., Livery Hats, Clerical Felt Hats,
Furs Altered.   Umbrellas Re-covered.   Silk Hats Dressed.

"AERTEX Cellular Clothing" from 5/- per Suit.

An even Temperature maintained in any Weather with

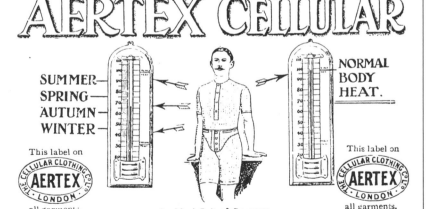

SUMMER
SPRING
AUTUMN
WINTER

NORMAL BODY HEAT.

This label on

AERTEX
THE CELLULAR CLOTHING CO.
LONDON

all garments.

An Ideal Suit of Summer
Underwear for 5/-

This label on

AERTEX
THE CELLULAR CLOTHING CO.
LONDON

all garments.

AERTEX CELLULAR is composed of small cells in which air is always
enclosed, forming a protective layer to the skin; while owing to the ventilated
structure of the clothing, any surplus heat and perspiration can readily escape.

"Pesco" and "Two Steeples" Unshrinkable Wool Underwear.

Hats set to the "Conformateur."

Chapter Four

Clothes

Clothes do make a man and even more so a woman. It's always been important to stress the fashionability of one's range, that you have the latest novelties. 'Novelties' was common usage in the drapery business, and seemed to be applied to anything new. Today, the term is more common in a toyshop or a gift shop, usually suggesting something funny, silly and probably pretty useless.

In women's clothes the passion for fur has gone, for the moment anyway. Fingering wool seems to have disappeared, and corsets, even self-adjusting ones which James Horn of Bridge Street, Appleby, was offering in 1869, have been adjusted right out of the market. (Did self-adjusting mean they did the adjusting by themselves or the wearer had to do it?) Cycling skirts have also disappeared, now that women on bikes wear the same as men, covering their thighs with the same self-adjusting lycra that fits any thigh, however fat.

The Victorians took funerals very seriously and Dixon and Watson of Whitehaven could offer the finest in mourning dress. Crepe is still with us, but in most old advertisements it was spelled as 'crape', which I presume is the same thing, and not some sort of pancake. If bakers could sell you domestic servants perhaps drapers sometimes threw in the odd bit of confectionery.

JAMES HORN,
STAY & CORSET MAKER
SELF ADJUSTING CORSETS,
Bridge Street, APPLEBY.

Directory 1869

UMBRELLAS AND CORSETS.

ULSTERS, WATERPROOFS, AND JACKETS.

HOSIERY, GLOVES, SCARFS TIES, &c.

DIXON & WATSON,

DRAPERS, HOSIERS,

HABERDASHERS,

AND

SILK MERCERS,

40, KING STREET,

WHITEHAVEN.

DRAPERS, HOTEL PROPRIETORS, HOUSEHOLDERS, and parties furnishing will find the goods sold at this Warehouse the Cheapest and Best in the kingdom.

Being supplied direct from the best manufacturers, we are in a position to sell every article at prices which defy competition.

Families requiring

MOURNING

will find it to their advantage to patronise this establishment. We keep every description of the best and most durable makes of Mourning required.

Very special makes of Crape, which we guarantee not to spoil with rain.

In the Silk Department

We have the best and richest Silks manufactured. No Silks sold will compare with them for quality or price.

We give each department special care and attention.

ALL GOODS MARKED THE LOWEST REMUNERATIVE RATE.

5 per cent Discount off Cash Purchases, or 2½ per cent Six Months' Current Account.

DRAPERY WAREHOUSE.

40, KING STREET, WHITEHAVEN.

SHAWLS AND FURS.

TODD'S
FASHIONABLE DRAPERY ESTABLISHMENT,
32, *Wilson Street, & Station Road,*
WORKINGTON.

Everything for Ladies' and Children's Wear at Moderate Prices.

The Latest London Fashions as Soon as Produced.

What Regent Street is to London, Wilson Street is to West Cumberland, AND TODD'S IS THE CENTRE OF WILSON STREET.

Enormous Selection of

Coats, Mantles, Raincoats, Dress Skirts, Underskirts, Blouses, Furs, &c., &c.

AGENT FOR MEY'S PERFECT FITTING CORSET AND THE CELLULAR CLOTHING.

HOSIERY AT KEEN PRICES.

| Everything New. | Everything Good. | Everything Cheap. |

Whitehaven News County Annual 1900

The most fashionably dressed women in Cumberland, possibly in any county, anywhere, must have been in Workington, according to the claims of Todd's the Drapers in Wilson Street - 'What Regent Street is to London, Wilson Street is to West Cumbria. And Todd's is the centre of Wilson Street.' No argument there then.

Whitehaven News County Annual 1900

Men in ads could also look pretty smart, whether in their top hat and tails or their ventilated shooting coats and scotch plaids, as supplied by John Boyd, clothiers of Whitehaven. Even riding their bikes wearing The Cumbria Rubber Co.'s celebrated Waterproofs, they appear ever so dashing.

Carlisle Rubber Co's
CELEBRATED
WATERPROOFS,
21/-, 30/-, 42/-.

36 in.
TWEED
CAPES,
3/6.

CYCLE
OVERALLS,
4/6
Per Pair.

A1 CLINCHER OR DUNLOP TYRES 10/6.
BAGS, TRUNKS, HOLDALLS.
FISHING AND SPORTING GOODS.
30 LOWTHER ST. CARLISLE
Telegrams—"Rubber, Carlisle."

Carlisle Directory 1905

Men's underclothes could be made to look surprisingly alluring - and bang up-to-date. George Tweddle of Carlisle in 1930 added a couple of thermometers to his advertisement, with some very confusing arrows, which were apparently to show that wearing his Aertex Cellular underwear gave you 'an even temperature maintained in any weather'. Even in

BURBERRY-PROOFS.

THE BURBERRY-PROOF KIT

Combines the indispensable essentials of Lightness, Warmth, Rainproofness, and is absolutely Self-ventilating

LOUNGE SUIT.—The most comfortable and smartest fine-morning wear possible.

GABARDINE COAT AND BREECHES.—For golfing, fishing, shooting, &c., in rough country; the best protection against inclement weather ever invented.

URBITOR—A light-weight presentable Rain-Coat for Town or Country

RUSITOR.--Never fails its owner; it yields blanket-warmth, is light, and by its weather-proofness endears itself to the blizzard-facing traveller.

SLIP-ON.—Justifies its existence under every conceivable condition. In fine weather it is the lightest cold-proof imaginable, and in rainstorms it keeps the wearer's skin dry.

Carlisle? In Winter? I don't believe it. But it looked impressive and scientific.

It's interesting how rainwear and footwear has often used science to sell itself - just like today. The latest climbing boots and trainers have always been tested in laboratories or contain new wonder materials. In the nineteenth century, vulcanised India rubber was the thing, or anything cellular.

Many of the brand names banded around are still with us, such as Burberry. Thompson of Kendal was agent for Dr. Jaeger's Sanitary Wool Company, a name still well known.

Back in 1864, T. D. Walker in Finkle Street, Kendal, had adopted 'the principles suggested by Dr. Camper (Who's he? I think we should have been told.) and successfully carried out by Dowie of London' (Oh, they were very good) and was offering 'shoes moulded according to the foot of human nature'. As opposed to dog or elephant feet.

Many of the shops and the brand names are still with us from the olden days. Bulloughs in Carlisle, which first opened for trade in Castle Street in 1910, is at present being run by the fourth generation of Bulloughs.

Arnison of Penrith is even older. Anyone visiting Penrith today, should look out for their shop, still in Devonshire Street. Outside you'll see an inscription saying 'N. Arnison and Sons, Ltd. Established 1742'. They claim to be the UK's oldest independent family-owned business. Not just a shop, a genuine piece of history. I'm surprised they haven't applied for a Lottery Heritage Grant.

Going inside, it's like a time warp, as if their 1930's stock was fresh in, their displays untouched since the last war. But of course, they have changed and updated over the years.

In 1899 they advertised that they had just completed a new furnishing department and were confident of continuing to be 'deservedly rewarded by the increasing patronage of first class families in the district'.

In that 1899 advert, they mention all the skirts, blouses and daintily trimmed lingerie they have in stock. They also said they were noted for 'Cumberland serges'. I wonder if any person, perhaps of the second class sort, was not quite able to pronounce Cumberland serge and found himself sent to the nearest butcher.

Messrs. N. ARNISON & SONS,

Milliners and Dressmakers, General Drapers, Silk Mercers, Hosiers, Glovers, Carpet Warehousemen, Ladies' and Gentlemen's Underclothing,

18, DEVONSHIRE STREET, PENRITH.

THE opening of a new and complete furnishing department marks a new departure in the enterprise of this old and well-known firm, who for many years have very successfully catered for the requirements of the local public in the lines specified at the head of this notice, an exceptionally varied display of the latest novelties and fashions in English tailor-made costumes, new styles in jackets capes, and waterproof long coats. They are also showing an extensive assortment of new patterns and shades in dress fabrics and smart silks and noteworthy specialities in perfect hanging cycling skirts, maid's jackets and costumes. The fine show-room is appropriated to displaying a splendid range of carpets, linoleums, curtains, soft furnishing goods and household linens of every descripton in medium and better class qualities. Messrs. Arnison & Sons' establishment occupies a central position at the corner of Devonshire with handsome and attractive window frontage. On the first floor are the show rooms for millinery, mantles, dresses, ladies' outfitting, etc. On the upper floor are commodious well lighted work-rooms. In addition to the more prominent features already indicated the firm have large stocks of ladies silk and cotton skirts, blouses, underwear, and articles of daintily trimmed *lingerie*, corsets, including the celebrated 'C.B.' and the renowned 'Her Majesty's' makes, hosiery, gloves, sunshades, ribbons, laces, and fancy drapery goods in infinite variety. The house is also noted for Cumberland serges, materials of the utmost reliability in wear, and justly popular for costumes, cycling outfits and other wear for both ladies' and children's garments. In gents' hosiery and underwear is offered an excellent assortment of goods of the best makers, and attention may also be directed to a remarkably cheap line in business shirts of faultless cut and style at 3s. 11d. each. The admirable catering for the public has been deservedly rewarded by the increasing patronage of first-class families in the district.

Cockermouth, Keswick, and Penrith Railway, c. 1900

5 & 6, GREEN MARKET, CARLISLE.

WOOLLEN CLOTH

ESTABLISHMENT.

DALTON.

GEORGE DALTON,

Linen & Woollen Draper, Silk Mercer, Hosier &c.

Wordsworth's Guide. 1851

29, SCOTCH STREET, CARLISLE.

STRAW BONNET, STAY & BOOT MART.

JOSEPH BLACK.

JOSEPH BLACK.
Woollen Draper, Clothier, Hatter, Hosier &c.
GENERAL WAREHOUSEMAN.

Wordsworth's Guide. 1851

FITZSIMMONS' HATS

FOR VALUE FIT AND STYLE
NONE CAN BEAT THEM IN CARLISLE

77 BOTCHERGATE.

Carlisle Directory, 1914

The Border Boot Repairing Depot,
AND CLOG MANUFACTORY,

4 & 6 Rickergate, Carlisle,
J. R. SPROAT, Proprietor.

Should you want a pair of Boots made to your measure, we can give you ease and comfort in either hand-sewn, machine-sewn, or riveted, and as for repairs we can make your old boots equal to new, as we are fitted up with the latest improved machinery, and efficient workmen.

A Post Card will bring us to your door.

We always have on hand a large stock of new and second-hand Clogs, including Men's, Women's, Boys', Girls', and Children's, and will make any kind of Clog to our Customer's orders.

MILLINERY AND DRESS-MAKING.
J. & E. ROAN

Beg to intimate to the Ladies of Carlisle, and its Vicinity, that they have succeeded to the Business of the late MISS WATSON,

63, CASTLE STREET, CARLISLE.

Miss R. having had eleven years' experience in some of the first Establishments in the West End, London, they hope to secure the patronage enjoyed by their predecessor.

Twilfit Corsetry

Regd.

ENGLISH MADE FULLY GUARANTEED

Fashions
Figures

MODEL 8535
A Corselet of Artificial Silk Striped Bastiste with the advantage of a Boned Uplift Belt to correctly mould the figure. Elastic Insertions on the Hips fastening at left side with Hooks and Eyes. Two Pairs of Good Hose Supports. Dainty Ribbon Shoulder Straps. Pink, 32—44ins.

PRICE— **10/11**

MODEL 3993
New Back Lacing Model of Soft Pink Broche. Two Elastic Gussets at Top to ensure a close fit. Out long over hips. Sizes 24 to 32ins.

PRICE— **18/11**
33 to 36in. **21/-.**

MODEL 1209
New Style in Wrap-round, Deep Fitting Back, in lovely Broche Cloth. Four Artificial Silk Suspenders. In Pink. Sizes 24-36.
PRICE— **12/9**

SPORTS 75
An ideal Sports Model with Fancy Elastic all round Top. Made from Blue, Pink or White Flowered Brocade. Fitted with Four Suspenders, Hustles and Unbreakable Spiral Steels.

Sizes 21—30ins. **6/11**

MODEL SPORTS 75

ROBINSONS
ROBINSON BROS. (CARLISLE) LTD.

ENGLISH ST.   'Phone: 854 and 855.   CARLISLE

HARKER & BELL

TAILORS AND CLOTHIERS

49/51 Scotch Street, Carlisle

TELEPHONE 528

Branch Shop—4 WEST STREET, WIGTON.

"The Leading House" For Boys', Youths' and Men's

Ready-to-Wear Clothing of Every Description.

— TAILORING DEPARTMENT.

All Suits to Measure made on the Premises.

E. RICHARDSON & CO.

TRY US FOR

Every Class of COOPERING.

If you are in want of a Good **WRINGING MACHINE,**
DOLLY TUB, DOLLY LEGS, WASHING TUB,
or any other Utensil used in the Weekly Wash, call at the
address below.

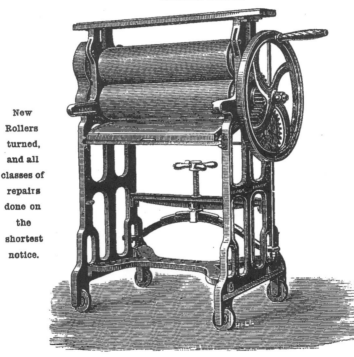

New
Rollers
turned,
and all
classes of
repairs
done on
the
shortest
notice.

Wringing
Machines
from
37s. 6d.

Small
Rubber
Roller
Wringers
from 12s.

All Classes of Coopering Repaired. Agricultural and Horticultural
Machinery of every description repaired. Best Materials. Best Workmanship. Send us your inquiries. Quotations free.

NOTE ADDRESS—

E. RICHARDSON & CO.,

Old Shambles, (Opposite Commercial Hotel),

HIGHGATE, KENDAL.

Chapter 5

Domestic

By domestic I mean stuff that you put inside your house, to adorn it or improve it, make it warmer, cleaner or just nicer.

Advertisements for any sort of new domestic appliance do lend themselves to strong, impressive, vibrant illustrations, even when it's something as boring as a cooker. The Gas Cooking Stoves supplied by The Whitehaven United Gas Co. in the 1890's look magnificent with all those pans and a kettle

WHITEHAVEN UNITED GAS CO.

GAS COOKING STOVES

ON SALE OR HIRE.

Cool, Clean, Economical. Always ready for use.

— ○ —

BOILING BURNERS — One Pint of Water can be boiled in 6 or 8 Minutes and 28 Times for One Penny.

Incandescent Gas Burners

Largest Stock in Town, including Globes and Fittings for same.

Superior to Electric Light and One-Eighth the Cost.

— ○ —

GAS GLOBES, GAS BURNERS, PENDANTS BRACKETS, PENNY IN THE SLOT METERS, &c

— ○ —

GAS FIRES

FOR HEATING. ALL KINDS & SIZES. NO DIRT! NO SMOKE! NO SMELL!

— ○ —

MAKERS OF

SULPHATE AMMONIA,

INVALUABLE FOR FARMERS.

— ○ —

COKE FOR SALE.

MAKES A BRIGHT, CLEAN, AND HOT FIRE AT LITTLE COST.

steaming away on top, fired by incandescent gas burners, of course, which meant that one pint of water could be boiled in six or eight minutes and 28 times for one penny.

And look at that handsome ringer available from

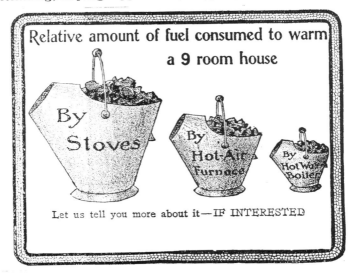
Whitehaven News County Annual 1900

Richardson's in Kendal. Don't you wish you could get to grips with it, give it a good ringing, or go into the outside washhouse and start bashing away on the latest dolly tubs. I sometimes think that in this modern world, all the sport has been taken out of washing. It might have killed your back but it meant that you didn't have to hire a personal trainer to work out.

Heating your home has always been a problem in this part of the country. Wordsworth and his family got round it on really dreadful winter days in Grasmere, when his lousy fire was smoking and they were all freezing, by going to bed in the afternoon. All of them together. Dorothy, his sister, tried to make one bedroom warmer by wall-papering it with newspaper.

If only they'd hung on till 1899 and gone over to Workington and used a proper heating specialist, such as H. Skidmore, M.I.H.E. Now he really knew how to heat a house - even a nine room house. His preferred method was a hot water boiler. It used hardly any fuel compared to the old fashioned stove or a hot-air furnace. His satisfied customers included Sir Wilfred Lawson, Bart., and Sir Musgrave Brisco, Bart. The Wordsworths would have been in quality company.

Or if the Wordsworths had still been having problems in the 1930's, Edward J. Hill in Carlisle could surely have sorted them. He lists all the domestic jobs he can attend to immediately, giving them his personal attention. 'You have a troublesome Kitchen Range or Sitting-Room Grate which requires attention. You require any tile hearth laid. You require an up to date Scullery sink fixed.' Then Edward J. Hill was the man for you.

One of the things about actual fireplaces is how they have hardly changed in looks over the last hundred years. Hewitt's of Victoria Viaduct in Carlisle, in 1930, had fireplaces which appear much as they do today, at least from the photograph. They were of course burning coal, as the tongs in front suggest.

The above illustration represents one of our numerous designs in Fire Places.
An Inspection of our showrooms will be appreciated.

R. N. HEWITT & CO. TEL. 403.

FURNISHING & BUILDERS' IRONMONGERS,

Today it would more likely be a pretend log fire, but the design lives on.

A lot of our domestic furniture has also hardly changed over the years either. Most of us still prefer wood, despite all the new fabrics and materials. And some of us still like things hand-made rather than manufactured.

Cockermouth, Keswick, and Penrith Railway. c. 1900

The better class of person flocked to Thomas Newby, cabinet maker of Main Street, Keswick, which is surprising, considering his shop looks so small and his range of furniture fairly limited. Nevertheless, he was 'Patronised by H.R.H. the Princess of Wales and all the Nobility'. Did he really mean ALL? He wouldn't lie, would he, or even exaggerate. It must have made Main Street very crowded, if ALL the Nobility chanced to land on him on the very same afternoon.

WHY NOT HAVE A NICE HOUSE?

When you can furnish at the lowest possible prices at the

Abbey Street
Furnishing Stores.

Every Requisite for HOUSE FURNISHING kept in Stock and without doubt one of the Finest Selections in the Trade.   Inspection invited.

Note the Address—

W. Donaldson,

CABINET MAKER, CARVER,
AND UPHOLSTERER,

12, 14 AND 16 ABBEY STREET, CARLISLE

Carlisle Directory, 1914

THOMAS  CORBETT,

SUCCESSOR TO   JOHN HUTTON,

Whitesmith,   Bell-Hanger,

AND BRASS-FOUNDER,
56, LOWTHER STREET, CARLISLE,

Manufacturer of all kinds of Kitchen Ranges, with Double Ovens, Revolving Shelves, Boilers and Steam Cooking Apparatus, Hot Closets and Bath Pipes, Smoke Jacks, (all from one Fire or separate), Pallisading, Gates, Invisible Fences, Game Netting or Fence, all kinds of Ornamental Flower Stands and Trainers, Picture Rods, Lamps, and every description of Brass Work.

IN BELL HANGING,

T. C. has greatly improved the principle, having erected an Apparatus by which he is enabled, at reasonable charges, to fit up all the Materials in a superior style, either in Bright or Bronzed Work, the latter of which he strongly recommends for durability.

Self-acting Slide Lathe-turning, and Screw-cutting right or left, and to any pitch, Machine-cut Wheels, Lathes, Slide Rests, Printing Machines, Printing Presses, and all kinds of Machinery Made and Repaired.

T. C. is Sole Agent in this District for

Perkins' Patent and other Apparatus

For Warming Places of Worship, Manufactories, Gentlemen's Houses, Hot and Green Houses, Baths, &c., by means of Hot Water circulating in Tubes, and laid in Coils so as to be visible or invisible, according to instructions.

The National Telephone Company
(Limited).

WEST CUMBERLAND DISTRICT OFFICE,
29, MIDDLE CHURCH STREET,
WHITEHAVEN

The above Company beg to draw attention to the rapid and easy means of inter-communication offered by the Telephone, and especially to the advantages of its EXCHANGE SYSTEM, through which conversation can be carried on as easily by persons miles apart as between those in the same Room.

The saving of time, and the advantage of having an almost face-to-face communication by a Merchant or Manufacturer between his Residence, his Counting House, his Works, or his Vessels in the Docks, in addition to being able to recognise the voice of the speaker, and thus know that the employee is in attendance at his work, is immediately apparent to anyone who has seen the Telephone in use.

Each Subscriber to the Exchange System has a Wire, bearing a number, running from his own Office or residence to the Company's Exchange or Operating Room. The Exchange is open day and night, and on Sundays.

CALL OFFICES.

Communication may be had with nearly all parts of Cumberland, and in a short time Lancashire, Yorkshire, the Midland Counties, and London by any private individual going to one of the Call offices, upon payment of a small fee.

LIST OF CALL OFFICES:

29, MIDDLE CHURCH STREET, WHITEHAVEN;
1, SOUTH WATT STREET, WORKINGTON;
LONSDALE DOCK, WORKINGTON;
40, SENHOUSE STREET, MARYPORT;
HIGH STREET, PARTON;
LOCAL BOARD OFFICES, CLEATOR MOOR;
MAIN STREET, COCKERMOUTH;
2, DEVONSHIRE STREET, CARLISLE;
71, ENGISH STREET,   DO.
WEST STREET, WIGTON;
164, MAIN STREET, FRIZINGTON;
MAIN STREET, DALSTON;
F. RICHARDSON, ASPATRIA;
VICTORIA HALL, HARRINGTON;
KING'S ARMS HOTEL, EGREMONT.

Quotations for Private and Temporary Lines and Inter-Town Communications may be had on application at

29, MIDDLE CHURCH STREET, WHITEHAVEN.

H. CHAMBERS, District Manager.

Whitehaven News County Annual 1892

89

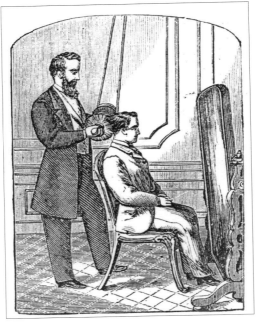

Chapter 6

Medical

But even more attractive looking than cookers and boilers were patent medical remedies and contraptions, especially the contraptions. Remedies, in the shape of pills, don't quite lend themselves to illustrations, but their healing qualities provided a lot of impressive prose.

In 1851, James Sawyer, dispensing chemist of Fisher Street in Carlisle had pills for almost everything, including 'indigestion, costiveness, flatulence, headaches, Loss of Appetite, Bilious and Liver complaints, &c, &c.' What was Costiveness? I bet I've got it.

SAWYER'S MILD FAMILY APERIENT PILLS,

For Indigestion, Costiveness, Flatulence, Headache, Loss of Appetite Bilious and Liver Complaints, &c., &c.

These Pills are eminently useful in most of the complaints to which the digestiv organs are subject, particularly in Bilious Affections, and a great variety of disease which are the effect of an irregular and imperfect action of the organs of digestio. They are safe, gentle, and effectual in operation—leave no disposition to Costiveness- nor occasion pain in their action, unless they meet with an unusual quantity of Bile ar Acid matter in the Stomach and Bowels. This circumstance will additionally recommer them to those of constipated habits, who are necessitated to have regular recourse a purgatives. In giddiness, arising from an oppressed Stomach, they give almost imm diate relief, and therefore put aside the usual but often unpleasant and baneful use emetics. They are also confidently recommended for Nausea of the Stomach, Acidi and other unpleasant symptoms arising from an indulgence in the luxuries of the tabl

IN BOXES, AT 1s. AND 2s. 6d. EACH.

SEDATIVE ESSENCE,

For immediately CURING the most agonizing TOOTH-ACHE.

This invaluable discovery relieves the most excruciating pain in the Teeth and Gum " and immediately arrests all further progress of decay," enabling the Teeth to be agai useful in mastication. It may be applied by any person, with the greatest ease, an having been used with success in thousands of cases, will be found efficacious, whe such things as Creosote, Opium, &c., &c., have failed, and being perfectly harmless t the Teeth, has one very decided advantage over the many nostrums which are dail advertised.—Ample Directions for use accompany each bottle of the genuine, whic has the proprietor's name and address upon the cork.

SOLD IN BOTTLES, AT ONE SHILLING EACH.

Prepared by JAMES SAWYER, Dispensing Chemist
23, FISHER STREET, CARLISLE,

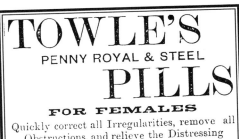

Whitehaven News County Annual 1900

He also had some wonder pills for 'Curing the most agonizing of Tooth-Ache'. He promised it would succeed where other remedies had failed, such as Creosote and Opium. Creosote for tooth-ache? I'm not surprised it failed. I've got some left over from the last time I did my old shed, but I don't think I'll try it. Mr. Sawyer doesn't give a name for his wonder pills for tooth-ache, or say what's in them. He just says he sells them in bottles, one shilling each.

In The Whitehaven News for 1900 there were some equally mysterious 'Pills for Females' made by Towles. They were said to 'quickly correct all irregularities, remove all Obstructions and relieve the Distressing Symptoms so prevalent with the Sex'. Sounds good, but it doesn't actually say what female complaint was being treated by these pills which dare not say their name or purpose.

Females of course suffered from many things which we didn't talk about - but in 1908, Jas. Irvine, M.P.S., chemist of Kendal, comes straight out and indicated what some of his female customers might be complaining about. '**If you suffer from Fits and Fainting**' so he announced in bold black letters, with no shame or embarrassment at all, then he could provide 'The universal tonic for Nerves'. This was called Bracene. He included a testimonial from a Mrs. Walling of the Nook, dated

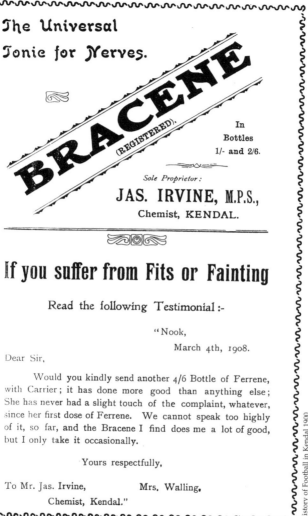

The Universal Tonic for Nerves.

BRACENE (REGISTERED).

In Bottles 1/- and 2/6.

Sole Proprietor :

JAS. IRVINE, M.P.S., Chemist, KENDAL.

If you suffer from Fits or Fainting

Read the following Testimonial :-

"Nook,

March 4th, 1908.

Dear Sir,

Would you kindly send another 4/6 Bottle of Ferrene, with Carrier; it has done more good than anything else; She has never had a slight touch of the complaint, whatever, since her first dose of Ferrene. We cannot speak too highly of it, so far, and the Bracene I find does me a lot of good, but I only take it occasionally.

Yours respectfully,

To Mr. Jas. Irvine,   Mrs. Walling.

Chemist, Kendal."

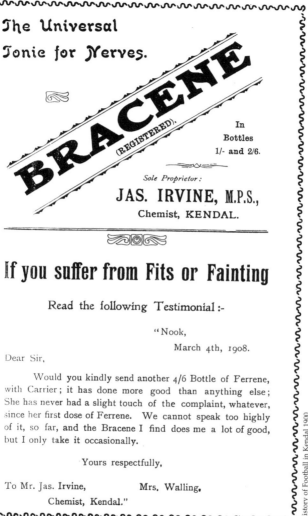

History of Football in Kendal 1900

March 4, 1908, who praises his Bracene. 'I find it does me a lot of good, but I only take it Occasionally.'

Well, that won't shift many bottles will it, if she's only using it occasionally. With Creosote, I bet you had to take it all the time to get the best results.

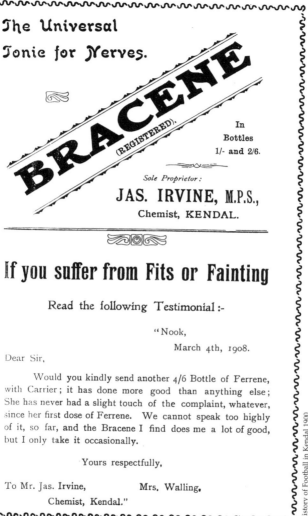

Dentists did a roaring trade throughout the nineteenth and most of the twentieth century. It was normal to have all your teeth out once any of them started playing up, and even if they didn't, just in case. Making artificial teeth was an industry in itself - and they weren't cheap. In 1900, Mr. Pettigrew of

Without Good Teeth.   With Good Teeth.

PARK & Co.,

KENT-DALE CHAMBERS,

Single Tooth from 2/- ; very best 4/-.

Upper or Lower Set from £1 ; very best £2 10s.

Whitehaven was selling a complete set of artificial teeth at prices between 21s. and 21 Guineas. That was more than the average working man earned in a year.

But, of course, they were worth it. Just look at that advert by Park and Co. of Finkle Street, Kendal, in the 1890's. It shows a woman with Good Teeth - and another, Oh Horror of Horrors, - without Good Teeth. Now that I study the illustrations more carefully, I think they are the same woman. Don't say the bad teeth were just painted in. Honestly. Some advertisers just can't be trusted.

Men were well catered for when it came to their personal problems of a tonsorial nature. Hair cures are as old as female

Whitehaven News County Annual 1892

pills and probably just as useful.

I do like the look of that Patent Hydraulic Machine Hairbrusher which at least two barbers in Whitehaven were using. One mentions it in his advert, without showing it, but John Taylor over in Tangier Street, includes an illustration, so customers would know exactly what to expect. It looks a bit scary, as if it might whisk you straight up in the air. Before you knew it, you might have joined Monty Python's Flying Circus.

Carlisle Directory, 1914

As early as 1914, you could avail yourself of a 'Certificated Masseuse' who would visit you in the privacy of your own home. I am absolutely sure this was all above board. No hanky panky. After all the Service was provided by the Carlisle Trained Nurses Home, telegrams 'Nurses, Carlisle'. They were respectable having been established since 1900.

"Lives there a man with soul so dead
Who never to himself has said,
As he knocked his corn against the bed,
Oh —— it."

IF YOU USE

SAWYER'S CORN PAINT

You will not use the unprinted word so often, but get rid of the corns.
IN BOTTLES, 7½d. each; Postage, 1d extra.

Sawyer's Tic, Neuralgia, & Headache Powders

Cure all Pains in the Head and Face. We sell more Tic Powders in a week than all the rest of the chemists in Carlisle sell in a year. Thousands of Testimonials.
7½d and 1s 1½d Per BOX; Postage, 1d extra.

SAWYER'S ASTHMA RELIEVER

Gives Relief in a Few Minutes. It is the Best Powder yet discovered.
Many say they would not be without it.
1½oz. TINS 6d, per post 7d; 3oz. TINS 1s, per post 1s 1½d.

SAWYER'S NURSERY OINTMENT

Clears the Head from Vermin and Nits.
3d per BOX, per Post 4d. Equal to any sold at 4½d or 6d.

All the above Four Articles can be obtained from the following Agents:—
Mr. HAYTON, High Street, Wigton; Mr. STRAUGHTON. Chemist, Cockermouth;
Mr. SKELTON, High-street, Maryport; Messrs. WILSON & KITCHIN,
Chemists, Whitehaven; or per Post from the Proprietor,

H. SAWYER, Chemist, CARLISLE.

RHEUMATISM

MOST COMPLETELY AND PERMANENTLY

CURED AT LAST.

TAKEN AS AN AGREEABLE **After Meals** TONIC. PERFECTLY SIMPLE AND SO HARMLESS that it may be taken by a Child in proportionate quantities.

The first visible effect of taking **MANX SHRUB** IS A Bright Face IN PLACE OF A SALLOW OR PIMPLED OR COARSE OR OVER RED FACE.

[REGISTERED]

Rheumatic Gout, Sciatica, Lumbago, Neuralgia, Tic, Face Aches, &c., &c.

(ALL MORE OR LESS FORMS OF RHEUMATISM),

Are guaranteed to be Washed Clean out of the Blood by

MANX SHRUB

Manx Shrub washes and freshens the whole body inside through the blood, just as the Manx Sea washes and freshens the body outside.

MANUFACTURED ONLY BY THE

MANX SHRUB Co., Ulverston, Lancashire.

DEPOT—RAMSEY, ISLE OF MAN.

Sold by all Chemists, in Bottles at 2/9 and 4/6.

Barrow Directory 1857

Chapter 7
Other Shops

If I were to go back in time and was wandering down our Cumbrian High Streets of a hundred years ago, wanting to gape rather than provision, I think I'd find myself heading for the nearest stationers. I do that today, wherever I am, but what fun doing it then, to study all the assorted stationery and countless printed delights.

In theory, we are all printers today, with our computers and scanners at home, national chains of shops providing our every office need, able to create our own personalised stationery, but

---

BOOKSELLING, STATIONERY,
BOOKBINDING,
AND GENERAL PRINTING ESTABLISHMENT,
34, SCOTCH STREET, CARLISLE.

T. F. WHITRIDGE

Begs to direct the attention of the Public to his STOCK OF STATIONERY, which is now complete, and cannot be surpassed for excellence and cheapness.

Cream Laid Note Paper in Packets, 5 Quires for 1s.

CREAM LAID ADHESIVE ENVELOPES, 8d. PER 100.

POSTS, FOOLSCAPS, BRIEFS, DRAFTS, AND OTHER PAPERS.

Ledgers, Day Books, Memorandum Books, &c., of every variety.

Inks, Pencils, Steel Pens, Quills, and every other Article in this department.

Wordsworth's Guide. 1851

Wordsworth's Guide. 1851

I feel the range of goods on offer was greater in the nineteenth century. So much of today's computer generated images are very much the same.

Even the smallest little local stationers could supply you with ledgers, accounts books, invoices, cheque books, pawnbroker's tickets, business cards, hand bills, mourning paper, all done in an endless variety of colour and quality of paper, along with quills, steel pens, slates, pencils, inks.

I can't decide, looking at all the adverts, if I would have spent longer in Pagen and Gill in Whitehaven, for it appears to have been a pretty big shop, occupying both numbers 1 and 2 Market Place, or gone to Carlisle to visit Whitridge in Scotch Street. His premises also included a select Circulating Library. These were once very popular in all towns, but the Whitridge Library does sound awfully select, offering high class literature with the very best of the critical and literary magazines of the day, such as Blackwood's and the British Quarterly Review.

John Reay, in St. Bees, bookseller and stationer to the college, could also supply 'all the London, Liverpool and Manchester papers' on the day of publication. Just shows you how quick and efficient the trains and the distribution systems must have been a hundred years ago. At Loweswater, today, I'm lucky to get the Independent by mid-morning, and even then I have to take my turn at delivering it. (I'm part of a rota that fetches it from Lorton, three miles away.)

Sheet music was also sold by stationers, and there was enormous demand. Gathering round the piano or getting out the fiddle, was about the only way of making entertainment at home in the evening. William Sewell sold music and musical instruments in Castle Street, Carlisle, and also Cutlery of Every description. Again, another strange combination. Perhaps it all began with musical spoons.

Jewellers were another source of fun and browsing for the

Wordsworth's Guide. 1851

idle window shopper. Johnstons on the Viaduct in Carlisle made a point of boasting about its enviable position and drawing power. 'The variety of their Stock is evident from their immense Window Displays which is one of the sights of the City.'

We know about pencils in Keswick, even today, but it's interesting to see just how many rival pencil shops and pencil manufacturers there were at one time. It was the Borrowdale

Mrs. JAMES CLARK,

Manufacturer of Cedar Goods and Black Lead Pencils,

The Keswick Pencil Depôt.

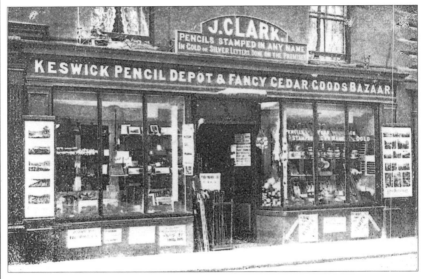

AN interesting and unique industry practised in Keswick is carried on by Mrs Clark, whose business, established in 1830, is one of the oldest in this special line in the Cumberland district. The Keswick Pencil Depot, situated in the Main Street, leading to Greta Bridge and Hall, has an attractive window frontage in which is displayed a large and choice assortment of cedar goods in a great variety of artistic designs, walking sticks, rulers, boxes, blotting pads and many other pretty and useful things adapted for gifts and souvenirs of a visit to the Lakes. There are also Frith's photos of views of the Meres and objects of local and historical interest in the vicinity, and a large assortment of the famous Cumberland lead pencils for office work and drawing and in various decorative forms in fragrant cedar wood with name stamped thereon. In addition to doing a large trade with visitors and tourists in the season, Mrs Clark also supplies these goods wholesale to dealers and bazaar committees, for which a comprehensive price list is issued with full particulars of the numerous articles obtainable from the depot.

Cockermouth, Keswick, and Penrith Railway. c. 1900

lead mines which started it all, making Keswick the national centre for pencils. Tourists on visits brought pencils to take home, just as today they might go for slate lamps or Kendal Mint Cake.

J. C. Clark in Main Street had a large notice over his shop front which announced he provided 'Pencils stamped in any name. In Gold and Silver Letters. Done on the premises'. You can still buy such personalised novelties today, with a girl's or boy's name on, but I bet they are never done on the premises. More likely to be mass produced in Taiwan.

If you wanted to buy or hire a tent then Kennaugh's Rope Paint and Oil Merchants in West Strand, Whitehaven, was the place. The coach and horses in their advert, to demonstrate the

Whitehaven News County Annual 1900

Messrs. J. B. BANKS & SON,

Wholesale and Retail Ironmongers, Plumbers, etc.,

MARKET PLACE, COCKERMOUTH.

sort of sheets you might buy to cover your wagon, are all gone, but their marquee, in shape and design, has hardly altered at all. You see such marquees every year at every Cumbrian agricultural show.

After looking at every stationery shop. I'd probably pop into the nearest ironmonger. Their stock was always enormous, filled to overflowing, with all manner of tools and materials whose purpose you could often only guess at.

The one I'd go to would be Banks in Cockermouth - opened in 1836 and still going strong. Like Arnisons in Penrith, it should be sponsored by the Cumbrian Tourist Board as it has become part of our local heritage and culture. Jack Jackson, the present owner, whose father started work in the shop in 1902,

Cockermouth, Keswick, and Penrith Railway, c. 1900

has even had national recognition, appearing on Down Your
Way and The Antiques Road Show.

Behind the main counter, the shop still has in use a set of
ancient mahogany drawers, 172 of them, all in different shapes
and sizes, containing 172 varieties of screws and nails. From the
ceiling hang many old instruments and devices, for exhibition
only, not for sale any more, which include about a hundred old
lamps and lanterns, some poaching nets and a set of handcuffs.

Banks of Cockermouth, blessings on it, is one of those
shops where you don't need its old advertisements to remind
you of times past. You just have to step inside.

Muncaster Bros.
Ironmongers,
57 Botchergate,
Carlisle.

THOMAS CAMM,
Rope and Twine
MANUFACTURER,
Quotations for every description of

Manilla, Jute, and Hemp Ropes
  (white and tarred)
Cart and Waggon Ropes
Plough Cords
Tapered Plough Reins
  (Italian and Russ. Hemp)
Adjustable Halters
Web Halters
Rope Halters
Yorkshire Halters
Cow Bands
Scaffold Ropes
  Do.   do.   tarred
Sash Cords
Box Cords
Clothes Cords
Hay Truss Cord
Coir Thatching Yarn
Tarred do.   do.
Tarred do.   Twines
Spun   do.   Yarns

Cart Nets
Hay Nets
Netting Twines
Upholsterers' Twines
Net Cords
Hammocks
Tennis Nets
Rabbit Nets
Long Rabbit Nets
Snaring Cords (tanned and
  plain)
Blind Cord
Mole Twine
Mole Traps
Bell Ropes
Whipcords
Hunting Whipcords
Cotton Twines
Cotton Ropes and Banding
Sack Mending
Hemp Twines.

Whitehaven News County Annual 1900

110

MUNCASTER BROS.,

THE LEADING HOUSE FOR EVERYTHING IN HARDWARE

We Specialise in :—

Household Ironmongery, Cutlery, General Hardware, Incandescent Gas, Electric and Oil Lighting, Builders' Supplies, Tools, Farmers' Ironmongery, Bee Culture Appliances, Tinware, Dairy Goods, Brushes. Cycles and Accessories.

Makers of all classes of TINPLATE and SHEET METAL GOODS.

REPAIRS in all Branches of Hardware, Plumbing, Gas Fitting and Mill Work.

57 BOTCHERGATE, CARLISLE.

Richard Sewell,
SADDLER AND HARNESS MAKER,
63 Scotch Street, Carlisle.

Horse and Greyhound Clothing.
—— ALL STABLE AND KENNEL REQUISITES. ——

Portmanteaus, Dress and Suit Cases.
Gladstone, Kit, and Brief Bags.
Hat and Bonnet Boxes.

Large selection of Ladies' Fancy Bags, Purses, Pocket Books, Attache Cases,

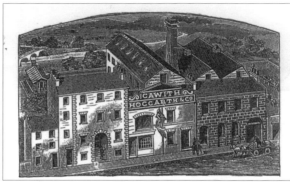

"The" Tobacconist.

Johnston's Tobacco Stores

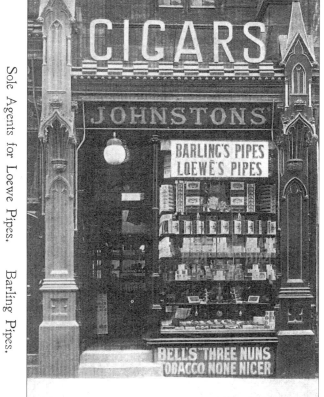

Sole Agents for Loewe Pipes. Barling Pipes.
Old Thatch Tobacco.

Proprietors of the Famous "Blue Seal" Cigarettes, 20 for 9d.
"Edenside" Cigarettes, 20 for 6d.

1 Devonshire Street and 55 Botchergate.

Carlisle Directory, Beaty 1924

HOLMES, Botchergate,

GENERAL DEALER,
NEW & SECOND-HAND JEWELLER, CLOTHIER,
Dealer in ANTIQUES and CURIOS.

Large Stock of Second-hand Gold & Silver Watches & Jewellery,
Diamond, Ruby, Opal, Sapphire, and other Rings.
OVER 2000 RINGS ALWAYS IN STOCK AT PRICES FROM
3/- to £100.

Gold Alberts and Guards in great variety, also Seals
and Appendages, Antique and Modern.

OLD COINS AND WAR MEDALS.
Splendid Selection of Solid Silver and Plated Goods.
**ANTIQUE SILVER AND OLD SHEFFIELD PLATE.
OLD CHINA ANTIQUES AND CURIOS.**

Gladstone Bags, Brief Bags, Hand Bags, Trunks,
Portmanteaus, Leggings and Overalls.

WATERPROOF COATS we sell much cheaper than any other
shop, Wholesale and Retail.

CLOTHING—Largest Stock in the City of **LADIES'** and
GENT'S CLOTHING—New and Second-hand.

Tools of every description. Cutlery and General Hardware.
Books. Opera and Field Glasses and Telescopes. Fishing
Rods, Guns, Musical Instruments, and other
Goods in endless variety.

Good Prices given for Old Gold and Silver
Artificial Teeth Plates, &c.

58 & 60 Botchergate,

HOLMES, The most wonderful Shop in the North !

Carlisle Grammar School.

An Ancient Public School with excellent Modern Equiqment.

HEADMASTER: F. J. R. HENDY, M.A.,

Late Scholar of Lincoln College, Oxford, and Assistant Master at Fettes Colle Edinburgh.

ASSISTANT MASTERS:

CLASSICS .... { J. HIGHAM, M.A., Late Exhibitioner Wadham College, Ox
{ Rev. E. A. POLE, B.A., Oxford.

MATHEMATICS & SCIENCE { L. H. BAY, F.C.S.
{ A. E. ELLIOTT, B.A., Oxford, First Class in Final Hon
{ School of Science.
{ W. T. STEPHENS.

FRENCH and ENGLISH SUBJECTS { E. HULLAND.

MUSIC and GERMAN.........REV. E. A. POLE, B.A., Oxford.

DRAWING ....JAMES ATHERTON, A.R.C.A.

VIOLIN ....J. CROZIER.

GYMNASTICS ....SERGEANT-MAJOR WINDELER.

THE School is in the outskirts of the city, and faces South and West. Boarders are received in Headmaster's House; terms moderate. Two Boarding Scholarships are offered annually in July. information as to Boarding arrangements, with Prospectus (illustrated), may be obtained from the Headma
There is a Playground and a Cricket Ground, numerous Classrooms, a Great Hall, a separate block Laboratories and Science Rooms, a large Gymnasium, and a Workshop for thirty boys. The First-c Swimming Bath at the City Baths is reserved for the School at certain times.
There is a Classical and a Modern side. In the latter a sound Modern Education is given, suited to who are intended for commercial life. There are special classes for boys preparing for the Higher Exam tions, such as the Examinations for Scholarships at the Universities and for Woolwich and Sandhurst.
There is a Preparatory Department, taught by Ladies and entirely separate from the rest of the Sch for boys under ten.
Successes of the past year include a Hastings Exhibition (Classics), and a Thomas Exhibition (Classics Queen's College, Oxford, and the George Moore Exhibition of £50 for three years.
The School is a special centre for the Oxford Local Examinations. 18 Certificates (Senior and Jun were obtained this year; details on application.

SCHOLARSHIPS.

TENABLE IN THE SCHOOL.—The Charles Howard (offered every three years), two Foundation Scholars (annually), and two Boarding Scholarships (annually), with sundry minor Exhibitions.
TENABLE AT THE UNIVERSITIES.—Two Thomas Exhibitions of £67 for five years, open to sons of clergy in the diocese educated at Carlisle Grammar School (vacant probably in 1900 or 1901).
At least fifteen Hastings Exhibitions of £90 for five years, open to certain northern schools which Carlisle is one.
Four Eglesfield Exhibitions of £80 for four years, open to natives of Cumberland and Westmor

For Prospectus (Illustrated) and other Particulars apply to the Headmas

116

Chapter 8

Education and Entertainment

If you read Cumbria Life today you'll see pages and pages of advertisements for private schools, all extolling their virtues, boasting about their academic achievements, their sporting facilities, their healthy situation. The words and boasts have hardly changed in a hundred years, though many of the schools have gone. St. Bees, the public school, is still with us, though now it takes girls as well as boys. Carlisle Grammar School, my old school, no longer advertises as it no longer

The School is situated in St. Andrew's Square, facing the church of that name, and was founded in the reign of Richard II. by William Strickland, who in 1400 became Bishop of Carlisle. In 1564 it was refounded by Queen Elizabeth. The existing building was restored about forty years ago, and bears an inscription above the entrance, and over one of the fireplaces are the Royal Arms of the Tudors. The school is governed by a Board of five Governors. Pupils are prepared for the Oxford Local;l Examinations, for which Penrith is an appointed centre. As the town is easy of access, many candidates attend the annual examination in July. Particulars of the Oxford Local Examinations may be obtained from the Hon. Secretary, Mr. E. J. Fairer, St. Andrew's Square. The headmaster is assisted by a staff of resident and visiting masters, and receives a limited number of boarders. terms on appl,ication will be supplied. The health and comfort of the boys are under the personal care of Mrs. Keed.

exists, as such, but is part of Trinity Comprehensive.

In 1900, the advert for CGS described it as a public school, which, I suppose it was, as fees had to be paid. It even had boarders, which I never realised, who boarded in the headmaster's house. Its list of masters with Oxford degrees was most impressive. Even the gymnastics master had a handle to his name - Sgt-Major Windeler.

It describes itself as ancient but doesn't give its foundation date, which I was told went back to the 1100's, when it was a cathedral school, but Penrith Grammar School - now Queen Elizabeth Grammar School - drew attention to its foundation in the 1400's. In 1900 its premises were in St Andrew's Square, facing the church.

Keswick School, then and now, took boys and girls as boarders. In 1900, Hawkshead Grammar School, founded 1585, was still in existence. This was the school Wordsworth went to as a boarder. In 1900 its headmaster was the Rev. R. M. Samson of St. John's College, Cambridge, which is where Wordsworth himself went on to.

Whitehaven News County Annual 1900

Whitehaven News County Annual 1900

Ghyll Bank College,

NEAR WHITEHAVEN.

Conducted by J. NIXON, B.A., L.C.P.,
AND
W. NIXON, B.A., L.C.P.,

Assisted by a good staff of Assistant and Visiting Masters.

GHYLL BANK COLLEGE was built expressly for a Boarding and Day School, in a healthy locality, at some distance from Whitehaven. The school and class-rooms are large and lofty, and well ventilated; the dormitories are large and airy, and there is a good playground.

The subjects taught are—Reading, Writing, Spelling and Writing from Dictation, and Composition; English Grammar, Scripture History, English History and Literature, and Geography; Arithmetic, Bookkeeping, Mensuration, Algebra, Euclid, and Trigonometry; Mechanics, and other branches of Natural Philosophy; Chemistry and Experimental Physics, for which there is all the requisite apparatus; the Latin and Greek, and the French and German Languages. The course of study is quite optional. Pupils are prepared for any examination, and an arrangement is in force by which boys, before leaving school, may pass an examination at Ghyll Bank College which will excuse the preliminary examinations in Law, Medicine, &c. The success of the school at the local and other examinations has been very great.

FULL PARTICULARS ON APPLICATION.

Whitehaven News County Annual 1900

Some schools then, as now, did not have a lot to boast about in terms of academic success. I don't think I would have rushed to send my children to Ghyll Bank College in Whitehaven, even though the classrooms were 'large and lofty and well- ventilated'. Your choice of which course to study was 'quite optional,' which could suggest it was highly progressive and modern, well ahead of the times, but I doubt it. 'Pupils are prepared for any examination' which again is a bit suspicious as no details are given. Unlike the grammar and public schools of the day, it did not list the names or degrees of its teachers, except to say there was 'a good staff of Assistant and Visiting Masters'. But prospective parents were re-assured that the school was successful. How successful exactly? 'The success of the school at the local and other examinations has been great.' So that was all right.

Cumberland and Westmorland also had several specialist establishments. Newton Rigg was well established, known in 1900 as The Cumberland and Westmorland Dairy School and Farm. It took pupils of both sexes, which sounds very enlightened, until you read the small print and see that Females attended from April to October and Males from November to March. Don't want them mixing. Who knows, they might behave like animals.

There was also an agricultural college at Aspatria, set in a most handsome building, which trained farmers and land agents and prepared them for the Colonies. They didn't have

---

THE CUMBERLAND & WESTMORLAND FARM SCHOOL,
AT NEWTON RIGG, 1½ Miles from Penrith Station.

Chairman of Governors: H. C. HOWARD, Esq.
Manager: Mr. W. T. LAWRENCE.

Pupils of both sexes are received. Girls (from 15 years of age) and Young Women from April to October ; Lads (from 16) and Young Men from November to March.

The ordinary course of instruction for Female Pupils is eight weeks, and comprises theoretical and practical instruction in Dairying in all branches, including Cheesemaking, the Management of Poultry, and Farm Book-keeping.

For Male Pupils the course is sixteen weeks, and includes Farm Chemistry, Botany, and Physiology, Agriculture (including Stock Rearing and Dairy Work), Land Measuring, and Farm Book-keeping. A Course of Lectures in Elementary Veterinary Science is given by a Qualified Veterinary Surgeon. There is also an experimental Fruit Garden. Fees, 10s per week inclusive for board, lodging, and tuition. Exhibitions are granted to suitable pupils by the County Councils of Cumberland and Westmorland. Scholarships from the Farm School to the Agricultural Department of the Armstrong College, Newcastle-on-Tyne, are offered each year. For further particulars and forms of entry apply to

C. COURTNAY HODGSON, Secretary to the Governors,
The Courts, CARLISLE.

Whitehaven News County Annual 1914

The ✣ Agricultural ✣ College,
ASPATRIA, CARLISLE.
Complete Instruction in the Science & Practice of Agriculture.

STUDENTS TRAINED TO BE FARMERS, LAND AGENTS AND TEACHERS OF AGRICULTURAL SCIENCE.

Preparation for the Colonies in Agriculture and Mining.

SIX FARMS, DAIRY SCHOOL, AND WORKSHOPS.
Apply to the Principal for Prospectus.

Whitehaven News County Annual 1914

too far to go from Aspatria to catch the emigrant boats at Whitehaven. From Newton Rigg, it was a much longer trek.

Music and Dancing Academies, however small, however modest, clearly had well qualified staff - as they always seemed to be run by a professor. Kendal had Professor and Madame Airey in charge of the Victoria Academy of Dancing, where 'plain. artistic and fancy dancing was taught'. Carlisle had Professor Chas. Dargan who taught the piano, organ and singing. He was clearly most accomplished. When he wasn't working on his twirly moustache, managing to get each end to a fine point, he was composing and writing his own songs. Some had a local setting such as '0 Bonnie Wetherall Woods' while others were of general if not to say eternal interest. I do

Yietoria Academy

OF

- Daneing, -

Entry Lane, KENDAL.

Plain, Artistic, and Fancy Dancing Taught. - -

- - Schools and Private Families Attended

 PUBLIC ASSEMBLIES
WEDNESDAYS & SATURDAYS.
(Open all the Year round.)

Private Instruction by Appointment only.

COLLEGIAN ACADEMY OF DANCING.
GAGE STREET. LANCASTER.
(1 Minute from New Town Hall.)

THESE ACADEMIES MAY BE HIRED FOR

BALLS, WEDDING PARTIES, &c

Being fully licensed and replete with every accommodation.

Principals :

Professor & Madame Airey

Members British Association of Teachers of Dancing.

Private Address : 3, LAKE ROAD, KENDAL.

History of Football in Kendal 1908

wish I'd been around to hear him sing 'The Last Goodbye to Mother'.

When people made their own music at home, singing no doubt some of Prof. Dargan's lovelier ballads, they needed a piano. Chas, Thurnam's in Carlisle, whom I always associated with stationery and books, was also selling pianos in 1900. Their advertising line was that having a piano was not just of use for entertainment - but as 'an educational factor in every household'. Today, that's just what they say about computers. Every child should have one, even though we know that all they do is play games.

If you weren't up to making your own music and

A Piano

is to-day an Educational Factor in every Household.

The greatest of care however must be taken in the selection of an Instrument.

Tone, Touch .Durability.

are the most important points to be considered, and upon which you need expert advice......This will be most cheerfully given, without the slightest pressure to buy, at the largest Showrooms in the North, opposite the G.P.O.

An Immense Stock, by the most NOTED MAKERS and at ALL ——— PRICES. ———

Chas. Thurnam **AND** Son

Appointed Sole Tuning Contractors to the County Education Committees of Cumberland and Westmorland,

WHITEHALL HOUSE
Tel. 107. **CARLISLE.** Tel. 107.

Carlisle Directory 1930

entertainment, then of course there were theatres, cinemas and shows to go to in all the towns, big and small in the county. Most of the old cinemas have gone - the Grand in Cockermouth is now an electrical showroom - but they live on in Keswick and Ambleside where the Alhambra and Zeffirelli's are worth going to see, not always for what's on, but just to admire the building and the decor.

Her Majesty's Theatre in Carlisle got all the number one

SOMEWHERE TO GO !

HIPPODROME

Dalton Square,

LANCASTER.

An Up-to-date Vauderville Palace.

EVERYTHING TO PLEASE

NOTHING TO OFFEND.

A Bright, Crisp, Clean Entertainment, **entirely free from** Vulgarity.

Two Performances Nightly, 7 & 9.

Popular Prices : 3d., 6d., 9d., & 1/-.
Pit.   Circle.   Pit Stalls.   Stalls

MATINEE every Monday at 2-30, 2d. 4d. 6d.
Pit,   Circle,   Stalls.

History of Football in Kendal 1900

tours, so most of the old stars of stage and screen appeared there at some time, including Charlie Chaplin. No need for Cumbrians to travel down to Lancaster, but people must have done hence the advertisement in Penrith for the Hippodrome in Lancaster. Could their promise of 'Nothing to offend, entirely free from vulgarity' suggest that our local vaudeville shows, in either Carlisle or Barrow, did neither of these things? I refuse to believe it.

Her Majesty's Theatre, 1928

HER MAJESTY'S THEATRE, CARLISLE.

CARLISLE VOLUNTEER

FIRE BRIGADE CONCERT

Patrons:

The High Sheriff of the County of Cumberland (S. P. Foster, Esq.)

E. STAFFORD HOWARD, Esq., M.P.
GEORGE HOWARD, Esq., M.P.
ROBERT FERGUSON, Esq., M.P.
Sir WILFRID LAWSON, Bart., M.P.

THE MAYOR OF CARLISLE (J. R. CREIGHTON, Esq.
Sir CHAS. FIRTH, Kt., Pres. National Fire Brigades Assoc.
Capt. ARMSTRONG, and Officers of the Artillery Volunteers.
Capt. BINNING, and Officers of the Rifle Volunteers.

A CONCERT

AND

DRAMATIC ENTERTAINMENT

WILL BE HELD

On FRIDAY EVENING, March 11th, 1881,

In Aid of the Funds of the Carlisle Volunteer Fire Brigade, which have been in arrear for
some time, in consequence of Expenses incurred in connection with the part the
Brigade took in the Welcome given to H.R.H. the Princess Louise and the
Marquis of Lorne, in Sept. 1877, on the occasion of Opening the New
Wing of the Cumberland Infirmary, and the Victoria Viaduct.

PRICES:—Reserved Seats, 3s.; Second Seats, 2s.; Pit, 1s.; Gallery, 6d.

A Plan of the Reserved Seats may be seen, and Places secured at Messrs. C. THURNAM & SONS', English Street; and Tickets
obtained from JAMES C. MASON, Hon. Secretary, at 16 Devonshire-St., and 84 English-St., and any Fireman in the Brigade.

☞ *Doors open at 7. Concert to commence at 7-45. Carriages at 10-15.*

129

Hayes & Parkinson,

JOINERS, BUILDERS,

CHOIR SCREENS, KENDAL PARISH CHURCH.
(From Notes on t'ie Parish Church, Kendal,")

Undertakers and Embalmers.

"Modern Arterial Embalming"

Involves **no mutilation or unpleasant operation whatever.**
The process is carried out by a **SCIENTIFIC ARTERIAL
INJECTION OF AN ANTISEPTIC FLUID.** Immediately
decomposition is arrested and all disease germs are destroyed.
The body of the deceased person can be retained in the home
(without any necessity for closing the coffin) until the day of
interrment.

Telephone: 105.

CAPTAIN FRENCH LANE,
AND
27, CASTLE STREET,

History of Football in Kendal 1900

Chapter 9
Tradesmen

Joiners were also undertakers, a connection which continues to this day, but it was on the undertaking side not the carpentry that they were able to boast that they were employing the latest most scientific methods. Hayes and Parkinson of Kendal in 1900 were using 'Modern arterial embalming' and in case you were not sure what that entailed, they spelled it out pretty clearly in their advertisement. 'Involves no mutilation or unpleasant operation whatsoever. The process is carried out by a SCIENTIFIC ARTERIAL INJECTION OF AN ANTISEPTIC FLUID. Immediately decomposition is arrested and all disease germs are destroyed.'

It was not always easy to understand why advertisers suddenly jumped into bold capitals, apart from showing off their printing skills, but in this case Hayes and Parkinson -obviously wanted to point up their scientific methods.

T. Lawson,
Undertaker,
Joiner,
and Contractor
Port Road,
Carlisle.

Telephone 11Y3.

Residence—
Clift House,
Newtown, Carlisle

UNDERTAKING DEPARTMENT.

Carlisle Directory, Beaty 1924

131

In 1914, in Carlisle, D. J. Hill, Monumentalist, was using letters of appreciation to extol his work on gravestones and memorials. His most satisfied customers were presumably the recently interred, grateful to have had a decent burial, but scarcely able to write and say thank you. Instead he used an unnamed Fellow of the Royal Society of British Architects who had written to say that 'now your tarpaulin is down and your work can be seen, it is being most deservedly praised on all sides'.

The truly up-to-date tradesmen were, of course, the electricians, gas fitters and plumbers who from the middle of the nineteenth century onwards needed to be continually abreast of what was happening and able to supply all the exciting new systems of heating, lighting, ventilation and sanitation. Even a little local plumber, like H. Atkinson, of 40 West Tower Street, Carlisle, could, in 1905, supply you with hot and cold baths and water closets, electric bells and zinc spouting and even lifting force pumps and hydraulic rams, whatever they were. He'd also fit beer pumps for you. Truly a master plumber.

In the 1930's Graham and Crawford of Carlisle ('No connection with any other firm.') used illustrations of their latest toilets and sinks which look exactly as they do today. How times don't change.

133

Coal, of course, was still in demand for domestic use, despite the arrival of electricity and gas. Binning, coal merchant, of English Street, Carlisle, was the agent for Durham and Yorkshire Coals - but also Naworth Coal. A reminder that in Cumberland we had our own local coals which came not just from West Cumberland, but from rural east Cumberland.

Wordsworth's Guide. 1851

Cumberland and Westmorland, being so rural, naturally had a lot of tradesmen and services supplying agricultural needs, from seeds to thrashing machines. Note that it was 'thrashing' not 'threshing,' at least in Henry McCutcheon's 1851 advert and also in 1900 adverts. It appears to have become 'threshing' from about the 1930's.

Carlisle Directory, Beaty 1924

135

Messrs. Mitchell's Auction Co. Ltd.,
THE AGRICULTURAL HALL, COCKERMOUTH.
(26 Miles from Carlisle.)

THE principal auction sales of agricultural stock and every other description of property, whether fixed or removable, are held in Cockermouth and the district by the above-named company, whose practice, extending over a period of half-a-century, is one of the largest and most important in the North of England. the business was converted into a limited company in 1873, of which Messrs. R. and R. J. Mitchell are managing directors, the former being also chairman, with Mr. J. W. Studdant as secretary. the premises occupied cover a total area of nearly two acres in extent, and are situated conveniently near the station, the offices included in a two-storey building providing accommodation for the clerical staff with private rooms for the principals, and waiting rooms for clients transacting business with the firm. Adjoining the offices is the Agricultural Hall, comprising large auction room at one end and accommodation for stock at the other. Outside the building on the Station Street side are numerous pens for sheep, and a spacious dining room is provided for visitors attending the [periodical weekly sales of fat stock, dairy and store cattle, sheep, pigs, etc., the Company catering in excellent style in the refreshment department. The Auction Mart in south street, which is divided from the other premises by a back lane, is a large and substantial stone building, fitted with stalls for horses, cattle, etc., with extensive open yard attached, furnishing spacious and convenient accommodation for the numerous lots of stock sent up for disposal weekly and periodically. In addition to their important business in the departments mentioned, Messrs. Mitchell hold frequent sales of shares and land-lettings for many of the chief owners of property in the district, household furniture, while they have also a great Spring Prize show and sale of saddle and harness horses, cobs, ponies, bus and cartnags, and in the autumn an extensive sale of saddle and harness horses, unbroken cart and harness colts and fillies, foals, etc. In connection with this branch of the busi-

ness a sale of horses is held every second Friday in the month. A great Spring prize show and sale of young shorthorn bulls is held in March, also one in the autumn. large and important sales of all kinds of store sheep are held in autumn, which include special sales of top lambs and pure-bred rams and ewes etc.

All these sales are largely attended by buyers and sellers from all parts of the British Isles.

Carlisle Directory 1930

Agricultural auctioneers, if they were any good., stayed in business for many years. Mitchells of Cockermouth, still one of the biggest in our region, began trading in the 1840's, becoming a limited company in 1873. Their stone buildings and auction ring were well-known in the middle of Cockermouth. In 2002 they will move to new premises outside Cockermouth, leaving Sainsbury's to take over their old site.

Laundries did good business, even though most middle class households had domestic servants who did the drudgery jobs. Laundries could turn black shirts clean, do bleaching, art-dying and carpet beating, and also seemed to think they were doing us all a favour. 'Let Carlisle Prosper! Help It's Prosperity.. By sending your Dyeing, Dry Cleaning and Laundry Work' to W. Brown and Sons.

That's an advert from the 1930's and the first I'd noticed where that naughty apostrophe has crept into the word 'its'.

Its commonplace today. Sorry. It's commonplace today, in local and even national advertisements, but in the nineteenth century they were very hot on good grammar. After all, we did have some excellent ancient Grammar Schools.

BEATTIE & CO.
SCULPTORS

EXAMPLES OF OUR WORK MAY BE SEEN IN ALMOST ANY BURIAL GROUND IN THE BORDER COUNTIES.

LATEST MACHINERY FOR LETTER-CUTTING, CARVING AND POLISHING.

CUTTING HARD GREEN CUMBER-LAND SLATE.

SAWING OUT CROSSES, ETC.

Largest and Best Equipped Monumental Works in the North of England.

CARVING BY PNEUMATIC TOOL.

Head Office & Works—

WARWICK RD., CARLISLE.

Phone———— 467

138

HEAD OFFICES : 21, MAJOR STREET, MANCHESTER,

Telegraphic Address:—"BEELA, MANCHESTER."

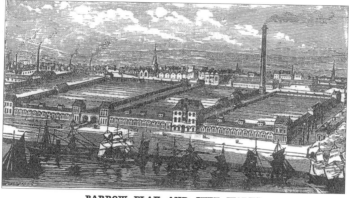

BARROW FLAX AND JUTE WORKS.

THOMAS BRIGGS,
SPINNER AND MANUFACTURER,
SACKING AND SACKS.

Sheeting, Canvas, &c.; Ropes, Spun Yarn, Engine Flax, Hemp and Jute Yarns, Cotton Yarns, &c.; Machine-Made Twines.

Hemp and Cotton Main Driving Ropes.

BRIGGS' PATENT LINED BAGS, for Coffee, Sugar, &c.

RAILWAY WAGON, CART AND STACK COVERS, COTTON AND LINEN OIL CLOTHS, PATENT TARPAULIN, AND PATENT PACKING; BRATTICE CLOTH, &c., FOR COLLIERIES.

Patent Dressing for Wagon Covers. Briggs' Patent Roofing Cloth.

Sole Tent Maker to Her Majesty's War Office, and Contractor for Government and Railway Stores. Sacks, Bags, Sacking, Bagging, Tarpaulins, &c. Hessians 18 inches to 108 inches wide.

8

Kelly's Directory 1897

GEORGE IRVING,

Repairs
Promptly
Executed.

Best Welsh
and
Westmorland
Slates
in Stock.

Estimates
Given Free.

Staffordshire
Ridge.
Laths, etc.

Private Residence—
15 BRUNTON AVENUE.

LONDON ROAD, CARLISLE.

The Best Laundry in the
North of England is—

The Carlisle

Telephone
389.

Steam Laundry

WARWICK RD.   CARLISLE

You want your Shirts white and spotless
You want your Collars Stiff and Immaculate
You want your Blouse to surpass its appearance
  when new
You have a Dress that wants Cleaning or Dyeing
You have a suit to Clean, or Dye, or Press
You have any kind of Fancy Goods that you
  are afraid to trust to ordinary hands

Send them to the Laundry !

Where skilled hands will make the best job that can be made of
them, in many cases turning them out like new. There is no
other place in the North of England so well equipped for doing
——————— High-class work as the Laundry. ———————

COME AND INSPECT IT FOR YOURSELVES

A Postcard asking for the Van to call will receive immediate attention.

DYEING AND CLEANING.

JOHN BROWN & SON,
STEAM DYERS,
FRENCH CLEANERS,
CRAPE DRESSERS, &c., &c.,
37, LOWTHER STREET, WHITEHAVEN.

Furniture Department.

Silk, Satin, Rep, Cloth, Damask, and all other expensive Curtains and Furniture Covers cleaned ; or, if faded, can be dyed and well finished.

Table Covers, in Cloth, Tapestry, Damask, Union Damask, and all other materials generally look well cleaned, or can be changed in colour.

Altar-Cloths Cleaned and properly Renovated.

Pulpit Hangings and Fringes Renewed in Colour.

Ladies' Dress Department.
SILK VELVET DRESSES JACKETS, &c.,

When not faded, and only crushed with wear, can be nicely renovated without being dyed ; if faded, can be dyed an excellent black and properly finished.

Dresses in Materials such as CASHMERE, REP, FRENCH MERINO, CLOTH, or other good WOOLLEN STUFFS can generally be dyed any colour; Dresses of inferior materials should be dyed black, brown, or violet.

VELVETEEN DRESSES

Look best in claret when not far faded ; otherwise they should be dyed maroon or violet. They seldom dye a good black.

LADIES' ULSTERS. CLOAKS, &c.,

Can generally be cleaned to look well ; or, if faded, they can be dyed dark brown, navy blue, dark green, or black, and sometimes grey.

FEATHERS.

Having made considerable improvement in the dyeing and curling of Feathers, J. B. & Son have every confidence in soliciting a trial in this branch.

COUNTERPANES, QUILTS, AND BLANKETS CLEANED.

FURS Cleaned and Altered to Fashion.

Gentlemen's Department.
BLACK CLOTH SUITS,

When not much stained or faded, can be nicely French cleaned and pressed, at a small cost, and on a day or two's notice.

FADED BLACK CLOTH,

Or Black Twilled Clothes, of every description can be dyed a good black and neatly pressed.

TWEED SUITS

Always look well cleaned, unless when faded ; then they can be dyed to look well in such colours as dark brown, olive, or black, and (if not too far faded and the cloth is suitable) navy blue.

Whitehaven News County Annual 1900

CARLISLE SAVINGS BANK

Chapter 10

White Collar Workers

The real professional like lawyers never advertised, didn't want to, not allowed to, till very recently, but there were lots of white-collar firms, whose job it was to give professionals help and advice, who paid to advertise.

The most frequent advertisers were those offering services of a financial nature. There were dozens of different Cumbrian banks in the nineteenth century, in towns and even small villages, offering savings and mortgage facilities. I knew most of their names from collecting cheques from dead Cumbrian banks, but what surprised me was the existence of stockbrokers. I had assumed, without really thinking about it, that they must only have existed in London and the big provincial cities like Manchester and Liverpool, yet, in 1900,

HALLIWELL & PORTER,
STOCK, SHARE, AND IRONBROKERS,
Commission & Insurance Agents,
13, LOWTHER STREET,
WHITEHAVEN.

TELEGRAMS—HALLIWELL, WHITEHAVEN.　　TELEPHONE NO. 23.

Monthly Share Lists.
Weekly Lists of Shares for Sale and Wanted in "The Whitehaven News," "West Cumberland Post," "Whitehaven Free Press," and "West Cumberland Times."
Exchange Prices Every Hour.
Quotations by Wire Free.
Every Description of Stock Bought or Sold.
Valuations for Probate.
Investments Insured.
Stock Loans Negotiated.
Annuities Bought.
Mortgages Negotiated and Insured.
Reversions and Life Interests Purchased.
Life Assurance.
Fire, Accident, Boiler, Marine, and Guarantee Insurance.

Whitehaven News County Annual 1900

143

Halliwell and Porter in Lowther Street, Whitehaven, were offering almost the whole range of financial services. They traded in stocks and shares, bought annuities, gave valuations, organised life assurance. You could even check how your shares were doing - on the hour. Who needs the net?

The services offered by local photographers were equally wide and extensive, even well over a hundred years ago. Photography began around the middle of the nineteenth century, and was originally cumbersome and expensive, but in just ten years, it had spread all over the country with keen, usually fairly well-heeled amateurs snapping away, followed by high street photographic studios offering portraits to the masses.

E Fowler Richards of Penrith was in business from the 1860's. His photographic studio had been patronised, so he said, by H.R.H. the Prince of Wales and H.I.M. the German Emperor. They did the hotels, bought the frocks, then had their photie took.

In Lakeland proper, there were many photographic studios who became very well known in their day, such as Abrahams, Pettitt and Maysons. Their mountain and lakes photographs, their post cards and picture books, are still admired and collected today.

In the more industrial, non tourist towns, from Barrow to Carlisle, there were dozens of portrait photographers who specialised in family photos on special occasions. You would dress up in your best and go into a specially arranged little studio which would be draped with elegant soft furnishings and fancy fittings, to suggest it might be your own home. They would even provide clothes and accessories, if your own were not posh enough. Then you would buy lots of copies to send to your friends, embossed with the photographer's name and studio.

Many of the photographic facilities on offer are just as good

E. FOWLER RICHARDS,

HIGH CLASS PHOTOGRAPHER, "THE" STUDIO, PENRITH.

No one will be found to deny that the growth and almost universal expansion of the art of photography has resulted in a general quickening of the artistic sense on the part of the people of this and other countries, as well as bringing works of true art within reach of almost every class. The fact still remains, however, that in photography as in other vocations there is a vast difference in the skill and general proficiency of its followers and that comparatively few are artists in other than name. E. Fowler Richards, of "The: Studio, Penrith, has been engaged in practical photography for over thirty-five years, and having always studied the subjects from a distinctively artistic point of view, the results attained fully prove the wisdom of the methods. The business has been carried on for nearly twenty years, and has brought the standards of execution in all lines of photography up to the highest point of perfection. "The" Studio is situated at the south end of the town, near the General Post Office, and is admirably suited for the practical work of taking and preparing photographs. The reception room, dressing rooms, and studio are all on the ground floor, this being found a great convenience to patrons, and especially to invalids, who do not care to mount many stairs. The decoration of the rooms is exceptionally handsome and in thoroughly good taste. A very fine and typical display is made in the different lines of work undertaken, including portraits of all sizes and styles, enlargements, indoor and outdoor views, etc., the collection being noticeable for its artistic quality and finish. Indeed, high class photography may be said to be the speciality of the establishment. All branches are undertaken and carried out with the best and latest appliances for the business. Enlargements of all kinds are finished in water colours or crayons. All sizes of portraits - cartes, cabinets, panels, etc. -are taken with particular care; children's photography, and groups, mansions, interiors of rooms, "at homes," and views of natural objects and scenery receive special attention, and the highest success has been attained in all departments. price lists and full particulars are furnished on application. "The" Studio, which, with the show rooms, is open daily, has had the distinguished patronage of H.R.H. the Prince of Wales and H.I.M. the German Emperor, and is also extensively patronised by all the nobility and the leading gentry of the district. We may add that E. Fowler Richards has done nearly all the photographic work in the Penrith district fo the illustration of the present volume.

Cockermouth, Keswick, and Penrith Railway, c. 1900

as today's, and just as quick. A hundred years ago you could have a snap of yourself produced on a Christmas card, fitted into a locket, put inside a broach. James Beaty of Carlisle in the 1930's took your photograph, made it into a block, then printed the result on your personalised stationery or post cards - all on the premises. 'We do the Whole Thing!!' Snappy Snaps indeed.

Tassels in Lowther Street, Carlisle, promised that films received by ten in the morning would be printed by ten the next morning. In photography, as in several other areas, most notably our postal systems, it's hard to see where progress has been made, despite all the IT and digital wonders.

Are journalists professionals? White collar workers anyway and there were lots of work for them when the country had four times as many local papers as we have today.

I have a copy of the West Cumberland News for 1931 - now long gone - which on its masthead listed all the papers it had incorporated:-The Maryport News, the Cockermouth

Chronicle, Workington News, West Cumberland Advertiser, Whitehaven Free Press , Whitehaven Herald.

In Carlisle, The Cumberland News still lists on its editorial page one of several local papers it has gobbled up over the years, the Carlisle Patriot, which first appeared in 1815. In 1869, the Patriot came out on a Tuesday, price one penny, and on a

---

THE "CARLISLE · PATRIOT"

(ESTABLISHED 1815)

Is Published every TUESDAY, Price One Penny; and every FRIDAY Price Twopence. With the FRIDAY's Edition is also issued a **Supplement,** which, with the "PATRIOT" of that day, consists of **72 Columns,** Price Threepence, or if Stamped, Fourpence—the extra Penny sufficing for the transmission of the additional Sheet and the Paper by Post.

LATEST

The "CARLISLE PATRIOT" has a large and influential connection throughout the counties of Cumberland and Westmorland; and, from the nature and extent of its circulation, is a most eligible medium for ADVERTISEMENTS. It presents an ample digest of all the News of the Week, and a complete reflex of Public Opinion, with an independent advocacy of Constitutional Principles. All matters affecting the interests and improvements of Agriculture, the extension of Commerce, the development of Railway communication, and the advancement of Industrial Progress, are duly published. The Church, and its institutions for Religious, Educational, and Social objects are earnestly supported; the LOCAL NEWS of the District extensively collected, and full REPORTS of all Public Proceedings impartially given. By a liberal employment of the Magnetic Telegraph, early information of Foreign, Metropolitan, and Provincial Intelligence is published, with the LATEST state of the Monetary, Commercial, and Agricultural MARKETS.

PROPRIETORS,

The Carlisle Conservative Newspaper Company, Limited,

WHOSE PUBLISHING OFFICE IS IN

ENGLISH STREET, CARLISLE.

Agents and Correspondents are appointed in the principal Towns of the district through which the "Patriot" circulates.

Friday, price Twopence. It had no shame in describing itself as a Conservative paper. Its 1869 advert listed their major concerns - agriculture, railways, the church, industry - four good topics for any local paper of the times. But it also covered non-local news. 'By a liberal employment of the Magnetic Telegraph, early information of Foreign, Metropolitan and Provincial Intelligence is Published.'

THE CARLISLE JOURNAL

(ESTABLISHED 1798),

IS PUBLISHED EARLY EVERY FRIDAY MORNING,

And is extensively circulated throughout the

Northern Counties of England and South of Scotland;

Especially in the towns of

Carlisle, Penrith, Alston, Appleby Brampton, Wigton, Maryport, Workington, Cockermouth, Whitehaven, Long-town, Annan, Langholm, Haltwhistle, Hexham, &c.

The Circulation enjoyed by the **JOURNAL** is by far the largest in the Counties of Cumberland, Westmoreland, and Dumfrieshire,

The average weekly issue being now

UPWARDS OF 3,200 COPIES,

And it is, therefore, a peculiarly desirable medium for

ADVERTISERS MAKING THEIR ANNOUNCEMENTS.

Moderate Scale of Charges for Advertisements.

TERMS OF SUBSCRIPTION,

5s. PER QUARTER.

PROPRIETOR & EDITOR, JAMES STEEL,

To whom Post Office Orders should be made payable.

PRINTING OF ALL KINDS,

EXECUTED AT THE JOURNAL OFFICE,

ON THE MOST REASONABLE TERMS.

Carlisle, December, 1850.

The Carlisle Patriot.

Established 1815.

The Cumberland County Conservative Newspaper.

For **80 years** the **PATRIOT** has occupied the highest position as an advertising medium in the North-Western Counties.

PUBLISHED ON FRIDAY MORNINGS.

One Penny.

Half-Yearly Subscription, by Post, 3s. 6d.

East Cumberland News,

PRICE ONE PENNY.

Published on Friday Afternoons, with Market Edition on Saturdays.

By Post 1/9 per Quarter.

The Popular Penny Paper for Carlisle, Cumberland, Westmorland, and Border Counties, and the Largest Circulation of any Newspaper Published in the District, being over

18500 Copies Weekly.

Scale for Prepaid Advertisements for

Words.	Once.		Three Weeks.		Six Weeks.	
	s.	d.	s.	d.	s.	d.
12	0	6	1	0	1	6
18	0	9	1	6	2	3
24	1	0	2	0	3	0
30	1	3	2	6	3	9
36	1	6	3	0	4	6
42	1	9	3	6	5	3
48	2	0	4	0	6	0
54	2	3	4	6	6	9
60	2	6	5	0	7	6

Other Advertisements Charged Scale Prices.

Announcements of Births, Marriages, and Deaths, not exceeding 30 words are charged 1s. 6d. each, prepaid ; and longer announcements 6d. a line. The name and address of the sender must accompany each notice. Remittances may be made in postage stamps.

OFFICES: 27 ENGLISH STREET, CARLISLE.
J. G. ELLIOTT, Publisher.

Carlisle Directory 1905

Another, even older Carlisle newspaper was the Carlisle Journal, established in 1798 In 1850, the towns it covered stretched north to south from Annan to Penrith, and east to west from Hexham to Whitehaven, which gave it the largest circulation of any journal in Cumberland, Westmorland and Dumfriesshire. Quite a boast. Not even the Cumberland News can say that today. The circulation in 1850 was modest, by our standards, selling 'upwards of 3,200 copies' but no doubt their subscribers were all AB readers who could afford the subscription of 5s a quarter.

The Carlisle Journal was still going a hundred years later, in the 1950's. I know, because I worked on it. It was my first job in journalism, during the long university vacation of 1957. I remember going on the bus to cover the Penton Sports, on the Scottish borders. During one trotting race, a horse galloped away out of control causing mayhem. I think that was the word used. Or similar. The Cumberland News had this scoop, but I'd somehow completely missed it.

I never got a by-line. Newspapers, whether local or national, did not throw them around as they do to day. And I only got paid for what I got in the paper - at the rate of 1d. penny a line. Can I have got that wrong? Seems awfully small, but that's as I remember it, what I've told myself.

I didn't keep any of my cuttings, alas, but I do have the 1850 advertisement, proof that the Carlisle Journal did once exist and that I didn't make it up.

Advertisements do have their uses, providing information, enlightenment and fun.

NOTICE TO THE ADVERTISING PUBLIC.

ADVERTISE your Business. Do not hide your light under a bushel. Whatever your Occupation or Calling may be, if it needs a support from the Public, ADVERTISE it thoroughly and efficiently in some shape or other that will arrest Public attention,— VIDE T. P. BARNUM.

MICHAEL DONNELLY,
BILL POSTER,
8, Friars Court, Devonshire Street,
(Opposite the General Post Office),
CARLISLE.

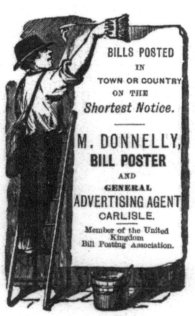

ADVERTISING SHOW BOARDS

KEPT IN USE.

BILLS POSTED

IN

TOWN OR COUNTRY

ON THE

Shortest Notice.

M. DONNELLY,

BILL POSTER

AND

GENERAL

ADVERTISING AGENT

CARLISLE.

Member of the United Kingdom Bill Posting Association.

Carefully Delivered & Addressed from Local Directories.

CIRCULARS

All Orders from other Towns by Rail or Post promptly attended to.

M. D. has the best and most numerous Private Bill Posting Stations in Carlisle.

Pic-Nics & Railway Excursions Contracted for on Reasonable Terms.

PLEASE NOTE THE ADDRESS.

Arthur's Guide to Carlisle. 1885